BASINGSTOKE
A Pictorial History
1935-1965

Basingstoke Town Hall in the 1950s.

BASINGSTOKE
A Pictorial History
1935-1965

Robert Brown

Phillimore

1994

Published by
PHILLIMORE & CO. LTD.,
Shopwyke Manor Barn, Chichester, West Sussex

ISBN 0 85033 899 9

Printed and bound in Great Britain by
BIDDLES LTD.
Guildford, Surrey

List of Illustrations

Frontispiece: The Town Hall in the 1950s

Acknowledgements

Although I am responsible for the compilation of this book, I would like to thank the people who contributed photographs and information concerning the war years: Mrs. Eileen Wolfe and Mrs. Anita Smith of Southampton, who told me of their evacuation to Basingstoke; Mrs. I. Hill, who gave me useful information about the bombing raids; and Mr. and Mrs. White for photographs of the bomb damage. My grateful thanks to the *Basingstoke Gazette* (previously the *Hants and Berks Gazette*) and the *Southern Evening Echo*, while Basingstoke and Deane Borough Council and Hampshire County Council were also helpful. This book is the result of some 40 years of local history research and over those years I have spoken to many people who have provided me with a great deal of useful information. My thanks to them all. But first and foremost I am grateful to my wife, Lana, for her patience while I have been putting this book together and typing it out. Her home in Winchester Road was demolished to make way for the Town Development Scheme so the whole operation of producing this book brought back painful memories. It is to people like her that this book is dedicated. If they had not lost their homes and places of work, entertainment, and worship, we would not have the Basingstoke of today.

Introduction

In the 1930s Basingstoke was a municipal borough and market town of some 15,000 people. Situated in the hollow of the Loddon Valley in Hampshire, Basingstoke had grown from a Saxon settlement by the river to a town which had expanded, over the centuries, to cover the hills on both sides of the Loddon. When the market place was established with its Mote Hall in the 13th century, it became the centre of the town and trade grew around that area. After the arrival of the Basingstoke canal in the late 18th century, and the construction of the railway in 1839, the lower part of the town also became a business area. By the 20th century the principal business thoroughfares were London Street and Winchester Street, and the two roads running north from them—Church Street and Wote Street. Other roads, namely New Street, Potters Lane, Brook Street and Station Hill, also had their share of shops and other businesses, resulting in an area of some half a mile wide being classified as the shopping centre.

The Town Hall, erected in 1832, with a new clock tower built in 1887, consisted of a justice room and other offices on the lower floor, while on the upper floor there was a council chamber and a spacious hall. The caretaker, who daily wound the tower clock and collected the fees from the market stallholders every Wednesday and Saturday, lived in rooms at the rear of the building.

Prior to the acquisition in 1921 of Goldings Mansion in London Road, the local council had their offices in the Town Hall, but by 1939 most had been transferred to the new municipal buildings. The estate belonging to Goldings was laid out as a War Memorial Park at a cost of £4,496 to give the local folk both leisure and sporting facilities.

The local council came into being as a result of the 1835 Municipal Corporations Act, which provided for four aldermen and twelve councillors, from whom a mayor was to be elected annually. In 1939 Councillor William Doswell was chosen, although circumstances were to make him mayor for a further two years. A corporation was originally formed in 1392.

Since 1885, when the Parliamentary Representation Act allowed Basingstoke to have its own member of parliament, the town was dominated by the conservatives, although in 1924 the liberals took control for one year with a majority of 348 votes.

The 1930s was a time for building both private and council houses in the town, with local builders constructing homes on land previously belonging to private estates and farms. In the early 1930s the local council purchased a large area of South Ham Farm, to the west of the town, to build 270 houses, while on the Merton Farm, to the north-west of the town, 209 houses were built between the Kingsclere and Sherborne roads, part of the estate having been started in the 1920s. Also in the early 1930s about fifty houses had been built along the Basingstoke bypass, which was laid down between the London Road and Winchester Road in 1931. These homes were built close to another development off the Hackwood road, consisting of 126 houses. At the Winchester Road end of the bypass an avenue of houses was built for private purchase, at a cost of £545 each.

This increase in housing came at a time when the town was beginning to see the growth of its industrial development, which had started in 1860 when the engineering firm of Wallis and Steevens was established in Station Hill. In 1898 the arrival of the motor works of John I. Thornycroft and Co. Ltd. along the Andover Road led to the further industrialisation of the town. Another well established company in the town, having been transferred from Chiswick, was the leather goods manufacturer, Percy Fisher in Kingsclere Road, who opened his business in Basingstoke in 1913, while along the Winchester Road the aeronautical instrument firm of Kelvin, Bottomley, and Baird had moved to the town in 1936. With these engineering firms were other businesses which had grown from small beginnings, such as the clothing manufacturers of John Mares, Thomas Burberry, and Gerrish, Ames, and Simpkins, who employed a large number of local women.

By March 1939 the pharmaceutical firm of Eli Lilly had completed the construction of its six-storey building high on the hill overlooking the town, just off the Kingsclere Road. Painted white and floodlit at night, it could be seen for miles. Out at Worting village, two miles from the town centre, was the retread firm of Auto Tyre Services, established in 1926, which caused some alarm in 1933 when its mass of rubber tyres went up in flames. The commercial life of the town was also active in the 1930s, while the retail trade increased as more High Street stores arrived to mingle with the local shops. In London Street Boots the Chemist's and Woolworth's had been in business since the early 1920s, while Marks and Spencer's was established in Winchester Street in 1934. In 1938 Montague Burton, the tailors, opened, with offices above, in Winchester Street. Two shop units were built, the other being used by the jewellers James Walker Ltd. Opposite them was the largest store in Basingstoke, Lanham's, which was acquired from Thomas Burberry in 1914 by Edgar Lanham, who died in 1936. His son Frank took over the store and opened further departments to encompass everything that people needed for their homes.

Among the many shops and stores were the leading banks, such as Lloyds, the Midland, and Barclays, which were built close to the Market Place. During the 1930s the increase in road traffic had become a worry to the local council and police alike, while parking of vehicles, both commercial and private, caused concern in the narrower roads. Even in the main roads motorists were leaving their cars in awkward places. One lady parked her car across the entrance to Mark Lane, where the police station was situated, so the full complement of the force marched down to the scene and lifted the offending vehicle out of the way, much to the amusement of the shopkeepers.

The fire service was based in the lower part of the town, in Brook Street, having been established there since 1913. In addition to housing the fire vehicles and equipment, the fire station also contained a large billiard and club room, as well as accommodation for the officers and men.

The cottage hospital, built in 1879, on the corner of Southern Road and Hackwood Road, dealt with all matters relating to medical care and casualties. In 1934 it was decided that an annual carnival should be held to raise funds to build a new hospital in Cliddesden Road and these events realised over £3,400 for it.

The town was served with electricity from the Brook Street generating station, which was opened in 1914 and cost £14,000 to build. In 1921 extensive work took place in the town to lay cables for the installation of electricity into homes free of charge. In 1933 the Basingstoke electricity supply was linked to the Central Electricity Board's system.

Water for the area was supplied by the waterworks at West Ham, which was opened in 1906 after the previous works in Reading Road was contaminated by a burst sewage pipe, causing the deaths from typhoid of many local folk. Gas came from the gasometer off Basing Road, which was supplied by the Basingstoke Gas Company who had their office and showrooms in Church Street. The gasworks was built in 1834.

Basingstoke's bus transport was provided by several companies, but the main one was the Venture, based in Victoria Street. With some 40 buses on the roads, the town was well provided for, but even so there were still country buses from Oakley, Odiham and Aldershot, among other towns, that travelled into Basingstoke with a constant stream of passengers. The Venture, begun in 1926, had a staff of 80 people, and boasted that by 1939 some 1,200,000 passengers were carried each year by their buses. The first regular daily bus service through the town was Thomas and John Wood's 'Empress Motors' which travelled from Worting village into the town centre and back at a charge of one penny per mile; the service started in 1920. Their first bus was a converted van made into a six-seater vehicle; then in later years they acquired several 28-seater buses.

Postal services were based at the main post office in New Street, which opened in 1925, having previously been in a smaller building in Wote Street. At the rear of the post office was the sorting office, from where all the mail was sent out to the town and country areas. Next to the sorting office was the telephone exchange, with about 500 lines in use by the mid-1930s. There were six sub-post offices around the town which also provided the public in those areas with a selection of groceries and other goods.

For entertainment the locals relied on the three cinemas and one theatre, and for those who enjoyed a drink of beer there were ample public houses and inns. In 1939 the oldest of those cinemas, the Electric in lower Wote Street, was having a complete refit for conversion into a larger and more modern cinema, which was to be renamed The Savoy. Built on the site of the swimming baths in 1910, it was one of the oldest cinemas in Hampshire. The Plaza cinema in Sarum Hill was established in 1931, while the Waldorf, almost opposite the Electric, was built in 1935.

The Grand Theatre, originally the Corn Exchange, in Wote Street, was opened in 1913 as a cinema and theatre, but by the late 1930s was mainly used for stage shows and plays. In 1925 the building was gutted by fire and had to be completely rebuilt.

Of the many public houses in the town, nearly 40 in all, some were over 300 years old, especially the *Anchor* in London Street and the *Feathers* in upper Wote Street, where the old beams emphasised their antiquity. In the 1930s those public houses were places of peacefulness with only the chatter of the 'locals' to disturb the peace.

The education of the town's children was based on the Education Act of 1902, which brought about the end of the Schools Boards of 1885. In 1939 work was taking place in Vyne Road, on the hill behind the railway station, to build a new grammar school, called Queen Mary's School, as the former Holy Ghost School in Worting Road was becoming too small. Along Crossborough Hill, adjoining the War Memorial Park, was the County High School for Girls, which was established in Brook Street in 1908 and moved to its new site in 1912. The original Board Schools of 1885 were built at Fairfields, a site to the south of the town centre, while Brook Street Primary School was erected in 1909. At the bottom of Church Street was St John's School for mixed children and infants, which opened in 1901 on the medieval site of Walter de Merton's hospice for aged priests.

Places of worship in the town in the 1930s were well attended, with the result that funds to preserve and restore the buildings were forthcoming when needed. The parish church of St Michael's, in Church Square, which was mainly built in the 16th century, needed repairs to its roof in 1937, and by the following year workmen were busy dealing with the problem.

Unfortunately one of them set light to the woodwork with a blowlamp and within minutes the roof was ablaze. The fire brigade managed to restrict the flames to one part of the building, the south aisle, and within weeks, to the delight of the vicar, Rev. Anthony Chute, money poured in for the repair.

All Saints' church, in Southern Road, another Church of England building, was built in the latter years of the Great War by the architect Temple Moore; while at Eastrop, to the east of the town, St Mary's church, rebuilt in 1887, was the parish church. The Methodists had two churches in the town, in Church Street and Sarum Hill. The former was built in 1905 on the site of another church, which was rebuilt at Cliddesden village, while the latter building was erected in 1902. The Roman Catholics had their church close to the Holy Ghost ruins, near the railway station, which was built in 1902 when it was thought that a large railway works was to be built in Basingstoke. It was constructed at Eastleigh instead, and the Irish workers' never materialised.

The Congregationalists attended their London Street church, which was built in 1800 then enlarged and extended in the following years. In Sarum Hill was the small church occupied by the Baptists, built in 1908; while in Wote Street the Immanuel church built in 1775 was attended by members of the Countess of Huntingdon's Connexion. The Salvation Army, who arrived in Basingstoke in the early 1880s in the midst of riots and fights, caused by their cries of 'Ban the evil drink', had their headquarters in Reading Road. They were a familiar sight at the bottom of Wote Street, near the cinemas, playing their musical instruments and preaching to those who listened.

For those of a literary nature the library in New Street provided a regular source of books, having been established there since 1928 in what was originally the Mechanics' Institute, where public education started in 1869. On the top floor of the building was the local museum, opened in 1931, the result of many years' work by several men who had a great interest in the history of the town. John Ellaway and George Willis became the two leading characters in the setting up of the museum, and to promote their work they gave a series of talks and lectures on the history of Basingstoke. When Mr. Willis was not at the museum he was busy at his jeweller's shop in Wote Street, where he also mended clocks and watches. On one occasion he was fixing the clock above the War Memorial Park bandstand when he fell off the ladder onto the hard wooden floor. Two men carried him over to the cottage hospital but he only suffered a few bruises.

This review of Basingstoke, as it was in the days before the Second World War, cannot take in everything about the many facets of the community. Its clubs, associations, establishments and other aspects of this thriving town are too numerous to quote in this introduction. It is hoped that the following chapters will give readers the chance to visualise how the local folk lived through those dark days of the War and how they faced up to the problems of the future expansion of the town. During those years from 1939 onwards it was a period of uncertainty, not only from the air raids during the war but because of the unpredictability of the years afterwards, when the Town Development Scheme meant so much change to their lives. This book is dedicated to all those who survived that period—they will not be forgotten.

Chapter One

The War Years, 1939-45

At 11.15 a.m. on Sunday 3 September 1939 the people of Basingstoke, like most other folk in the country, gathered round their wirelesses to listen to the Prime Minister, Neville Chamberlain, make a special announcement:

> This morning the British Ambassador in Berlin handed the German Government a final Note stating that unless we heard from them by eleven o'clock that they were prepared at once to withdraw their troops from Poland a state of war would exist between us. I have to tell you now that no such undertaking has been received, and that consequently this country is at War with Germany ...

That statement had a profound effect on all those who heard it, and, although Mr. Chamberlain continued to tell the millions of listeners his thoughts on the matter, there were many who were too stunned to remember afterwards what he said. For a few minutes after the Prime Minister had spoken a great silence fell upon the land, as people thought about the consequences of another world war 21 years after the previous one had ended. Then the air raid siren sounded across the Home Counties, and, fearing that Hitler had already started his invasion of Britain, people hurried to their shelters. But it was a false alarm— a lone aeroplane had been sighted crossing the English Channel and a full alert had been sounded. Within minutes the all-clear was given and everyone returned to their homes. For eight months all was quiet—it was the 'Phoney War'.

When the expected air raids did not materialise, the public began to relax and some of the restrictions imposed on them were lifted. But certain Air Raid Wardens in the town did not neglect their duties during the hours of darkness. When they saw a light shining through gaps in the window blinds of local houses and shops they soon told the occupiers to 'put that light out'. It was evident that the local authorities had everything under control in readiness for war. Across the town First Aid posts were set up, the main one being at the Grand Theatre in Wote Street. Room was found in the cellar to house equipment and other items needed to help those injured in any bomb attacks. The Air Raid Precautions headquarters was established at Brinkletts Hall in Winchester Road, while the recently-built car park was used as an auxiliary fire station, a warden's post, and ambulance and first aid parties depot, and a mobile first aid unit depot. Opposite the fire station, in Brook Street, a large hut was used as temporary quarters to house the extra men needed to operate the fire equipment. At various local builders' yards rescue party depots were set up, while at the Town Yard, in Basing Road, where the local council kept its vehicles, space was found for a cleansing station in case of gas attacks, as well as a small depot for ambulances, decontamination squads and a warden's post.

Before all this preparation there had been air raid precaution exercises and a black-out practice. A.R.P. posts were set up around the town where people could get information and collect their gas masks. Altogether there were 12 of these posts in the borough, including one at Worting village. The transport services had previously made arrangements in the area in case of war, and for the first weeks in September 1939, local folk found that there were very few buses and trains. The bus service, Venture Ltd., stopped bookings for tours and took buses off their usual routes to be used for evacuation purposes. During the week before war was declared about 1,300 patients were evacuated from Park Prewett Mental Home, north of the town, to various places around the country. This was to allow the huge complex of buildings to be used as a hospital for wartime casualties, having been taken over by the Ministry of Health who provided 2,000 beds for both civilian and service casualties. Rooksdown House, part of the Park Prewett estate, then used as a nurses' home, was also emptied and acquired as a hospital for plastic surgery, with the eminent pioneer, Sir Harold Gillies, in charge. Born in 1882, this New Zealand surgeon experimented in replacing burnt and damaged skin with fresh skin after reading of the work carried out by a French surgeon in the early 19th century. After Gillies published a report of his successful attempts this skill became a recognised branch of medicine and he was knighted in 1930 for his work in this field. Another expert in plastic surgery, Archibald MacIndoe, who was born in 1900 and also came from New Zealand, helped Sir Harold in his work at Rooksdown although most of his time was spent at the Queen Victoria Hospital in East Grinstead during the following years.

The main evacuation scheme involved the transport of schoolchildren from areas at risk from enemy bombing to places further inland, and Basingstoke was considered to be a safe town. The government evacuation scheme began on 1 September when the Basingstoke town council was asked to provide accommodation for 4,000 children, expectant mothers, and other people, from places such as Portsmouth, Southampton and London. On arrival at Basingstoke railway station, they were ushered into the nearby cattle market to be handed food and for arrangements to be made to house them in the town. Various voluntary groups helped in this work, and transport was arranged to take the children to the homes to which the evacuees had been designated. Altogether 900 children arrived in Basingstoke, but there was no problem in finding accommodation for them, as over 2,000 offers had been received. Of the many children who arrived 11-year-old Eileen Foley, with her brother and sister, found the experience of moving from her home at Woolston, Southampton, rather awesome. They were accommodated in separate homes at Old Basing village and went to a mixed school close by. Their mother visited them on a regular basis, but she suffered the tragic loss of her parents in an air raid on Southampton, although her house was not damaged at all, and this added to her loneliness. Another child, Anita Gilroy, who was only four years old and also came from Southampton, had her two brothers and sister with her. They were also taken to Old Basing, and it was here that she spent the 'happiest days of her life'. Her home, in Mortimer Road, Southampton, was also undamaged by bombs. She was to stay at Old Basing for six years, during which she had an enjoyable childhood but experienced the desperate plight of the rationing scheme. On one occasion a lorry laden with food overturned on the main London Road, close to where she was living, and within minutes local folk were picking up the goods scattered across the road and taking them away for their own use.

For local children the day after war broke out was supposed to be the day they returned to school after the summer holiday, but instead arrangements had to be made to decide on what action each school was to take, especially with so many evacuees in the town. At Fairfields School a special meeting was held, while workmen rushed around to stick tape across the large windows, to stop the glass breaking in case of bomb attacks. The stone crosses, built in 1886 on the roof, were removed in case any bomb blast should topple them. The new term eventually began at Fairfields on 11 September.

Before the onslaught of the Battle of Britain some local builders advertised that they had materials, such as sheets of wood and corrugated metal, with which to build air raid shelters. Many people sacrificed their lawns to build shelters, while others started to 'Dig for Victory' and plant vegetables in case food became scarce in the shops. For those who lived in the lower part of the town underground shelters had to be abandoned quickly as springs deep down began to filter through and flood them.

The government realised that without adequate food no one could work properly, so a rationing scheme was set up, which came into operation 18 weeks after the outbreak of war. Local grocers and butchers had to make sure that everyone got their fair share of food, but a few gave extra to their regular customers. The first commodities to be restricted were butter (four ounces), sugar (twelve ounces), and bacon (four ounces), per person per week. As further items were added so people began to buy dried eggs, carrots and other common food that went into the making of puddings and sandwiches. Some folk began to breed chickens, which brought in eggs and meat, but their neighbours were not too happy with the noise of the clucking and regular rooster crowing. Quite often they were given a free supply of eggs to stop the complaints. On top of rationing the government brought in purchase tax, which was imposed on a vast range of consumer goods to check on consumption of essential war materials. It brought a great deal of criticism from shopkeepers, as it added to their wartime worries.

In April 1940 the Phoney War came to an end. With the allied troops retreating from Hitler's advancing forces in Norway and Denmark, Britain came within bombing range of the Germans. On 12 May the Germans entered France and by 14 June they had occupied Paris. The British government then realised that the 'safe' havens in Southern England were now danger zones for both evacuees and residents alike. Thousands of people had to be evacuated further inland to avoid the expected air raids. On 14 May 1940 Anthony Eden broadcast an appeal for Local Defence Volunteers to defend the country against the invading Germans. With the Western Front slowly crumbling and the war raging just across the English Channel, it seemed only a matter of weeks before the enemy would attempt to cross the sea. Within days the Basingstoke police station had collected a list of volunteers for this new force, most of them middle-aged or elderly as the majority of younger men had been called up to fight in the Army, Navy and Air Force. Throughout the country over a million men enlisted for the L.D.V., and by early July 1940 there were units established to guard and protect important buildings and places, the only weapons available in some areas being swords, cudgels and pitchforks. Eventually they received guns and rifles and the force was renamed the 'Home Guard', at the suggestion of Winston Churchill, the new Prime Minister.

The Basingstoke area had to contend with road blocks, which restricted vehicles, while pillboxes, most built out of bricks and cement, overlooked the main roads, enabling the military to keep an eye on vehicle movement and from where they could fire their guns on enemy invaders. Open spaces, such as fields, were strewn with large obstacles, such as tree trunks and old farm vehicles, to deter German gliders. Another feature was the disappearance of most direction signs, both on the roads and the railways. Travelling down from London, people had to count how many stations they had passed to make sure they were at Basingstoke. With the noise of the steam engine not everyone heard the name being called out. One person finished up in Bournemouth and had to get another train back to Basingstoke.

The air offensive against Britain began in full force on 8 August 1940. From then until the 19th, when there was a temporary lull, German bombers continuously attacked aerodromes, dockyards and munition works in Southern England. During that period the Germans lost 711 aeroplanes over Britain compared with 156 British. Three German 'Luftflotten', or air fleets, took part in the operations against Britain, with a total of some 3,500 aircraft taking part, including 250 dive-bombers, 1,000 long-range bombers, and 1,000 fighters. The Germans had over four hundred airfields scattered throughout Western Europe, including Norway, Denmark and France, following the invasion of these countries.

In Hampshire, bases were set up to defend both residential areas and military establishments, such as at Bramley, five miles from Basingstoke, where eight anti-aircraft guns stood waiting to blast the Luftwaffe out of the sky. At Winchester an observer centre was set up to watch for aircraft approaching from the English Channel.

During July and early August 1940 the Germans attacked ports along the coast, sinking and damaging large numbers of vessels. Then on 15 August the Battle of Britain began in earnest. Salvo after salvo rained down on various airfields in southern England and continued to do so the following week. In the midst of all this bombing Basingstoke was very vulnerable, and on 16 August the inevitable happened. In the late afternoon about ten J88 German aircraft swooped out of the clouds and passed from south to north over the town. Seeing the large railway goods yard they decided to drop a stick of bombs, but their aim was poor and the bombs fell into the heart of the town, while others fell in Burgess Road, north of the railway line. Then they flew off. Although the air raid siren had sounded, the residents of Church Square continued to carry on their daily routine, unaware that above them the enemy were about to make them homeless. The explosions shook the centre of the town, bringing people to their doors, wondering where the bombs had fallen. One young lad ran from his home to the scene of the attack with his mother screaming at him to come back! When he got to Church Square he was quickly ushered back by the police and other emergency services who had arrived there immediately. The scene was one of devastation. Many of the 18th- and 19th-century houses opposite the parish church had been shattered by the blast from three bombs that hit the ground, whilst the windows of St Michael's Church had been blown in. The Methodist Church in Church Street had its frontage badly damaged and its organ destroyed by the blast from the bomb that fell in Church Street. The crater that resulted quickly filled up with water from a ruptured main, and a cyclist who came charging down the road failed to spot the danger in his excitement and road up to his neck in the murky water. The bomb also killed a young lady as she ran out of her father's shop to give aid to any injured people. Altogether 11 people died in the Church Square bombing, while in Burgess Road several houses were destroyed, and four people were killed. One of the houses belonged to George Willis, the curator of the local museum and an alderman of the town, who was fortunately not at home at the time.

In Church Square, rescue work went on for several hours to make sure that everyone was accounted for. Several children were trapped in the sick bay at Dr. Leslie Housden's surgery, and one of them sang songs to comfort the others. It had a heart-warming effect on the rescuers as well. In nearby Church Lane many houses were badly damaged, and one lady was so badly injured that it was thought she would not survive, but she lived to tell her harrowing tale. In Basingstoke it was the worst bombing of the war, even though further raids were to take place.

Just over a month later another bomb attack shook the town, this time in Cliddesden Road where St Vincent's, a private school, was hit. It happened when the majority of the children were playing over at the War Memorial Park but unfortunately two ladies died in the explosion.

On 14 November Coventry was blitzed and almost flattened; its population of 213,000 were subjected to an all night bombardment in which 554 lives were lost. As the bombers flew across Hampshire to reach the city they dropped silver foil strips and other items in a bid to stop messages being sent to the Coventry area to warn of the air attack. These items, described as being like 'piano keys', were quickly swept up by local council workers. During the following weeks other bombs fell on the town, damaging buildings in Solbys Road, Southend Road and Rochford Road. On 23 November 1940 the houses in Bramblys Grange and Penrith Road were badly shaken by a bomb that fell next to an electricity supply building in Budd's Meadow. Shrapnel flew across the road, and the blast shattered windows in the houses opposite and lifted the roofs of others. One house had its curtains pinned under the roof as it fell back into place, with the result that the occupant had to cut the material and replace them. That same evening a bomb exploded on the lawn of the Church Street rectory, causing a crater so large that it took some time to fill in. The local vicar was 'more than pleased' when parishioners helped to shovel the earth back into the hole.

With so many men having been called up it was hoped that their absence would mean a reduction in the amount of crime in England. For a while the police found that the criminal fraternity had declined in the towns and cities, but it also soon became clear that many of them had fled to the countryside, where petty offences had increased.

Some local schools became involved in various projects to raise money for the war effort, while others corresponded with troops in various parts of the world. At the High School, in Crossborough Hill, the girls knitted garments for the forces, such as socks and gloves. The school also adopted the ship SS *Koolga* and sent the sailors letters and other items. The pupils were also taught first aid in case they were needed to help anyone who was injured, which came in useful in December 1940 when several incendiary bombs fell on the school, although no damage was done. Air raid shelters had been supplied for the school to house a maximum number of 217 people. Unfortunately there were 253 in the school!

Like everyone else in the country, the people of Basingstoke were supplied with gasmasks in case the Germans attacked with gas. But there was not one such attack in the whole of Britain throughout the war. The scare was brought about by chemical attacks during the First World War when both the British and Germans used gas while fighting in the French trenches. People in Basingstoke carried their gasmasks wherever they went, whether to work or to the cinema. Eventually, when they realised that the gasmasks would not be needed, they left the awkward-shaped box and mask at home. A few still carried the boxes around with them—but it would often only contain their sandwiches. The black-out which was enforced on people in the early years of the war cost some of the local firms a great deal of money in shutters and blinds to prevent the lights being seen outside. At Wallis and Steevens factory the skylights caused problems, and at the Brook Street Brewery it was months before every chink of light was covered. Park Prewett hospital had to order 3,000 blinds to fit their windows, while at Thornycroft's factory many of the windows were blacked out. Appeals to save electricity were often ignored. One business lady was prosecuted and fined £1 for leaving her office light on for 16 hours. The Corporation Electricity Department in Church Street asked consumers to use electricity only between 8 a.m. and 1 p.m. daily, to maintain supplies for the war effort, but this proved difficult for some people. Work had to continue through the winter months even though the firms were criticised for doing so.

The rationing scheme, brought in at the beginning of the war, had clothes added to it in June 1941. The ration book system of points, issued by the government, allowed people to buy the equivalent of a complete new outfit every year. This worked when operated correctly, but one or two local businessmen allowed their customers clothes and materials without the necessary clothing coupons, or accepted the coupons before the valid date. One outfitter was caught in April 1943 and fined over £5 at the local court to deter others from committing the same offence.

Petrol was also rationed, which restricted driving, thus causing problems for customers who bought goods in shops for delivery straight to their homes. Petrol cans also became scarce, as many motorists stored their petrol in sheds and garages, so some local garages announced that for every can handed in three shillings would be paid. One local character stole a dozen cans from a garage in the town centre and sold them to another. However, his next attempt was thwarted when he found that the garage, where he had stolen the cans, now had its name stamped on them!

Several people were caught by the police for using their cars for inessential outings and were taken to court. One businessman was fined £2 for taking his child to school in his car, after taking petrol from his firm's allowance. In February 1943 it was announced that a rationalisation of milk deliveries would take place, to save petrol. Various dairies in the Basingstoke area pooled their resources and arranged that only one vehicle would deliver milk in each road. Prior to this the local dairies had amalgamated into the Hampshire Dairies Ltd. in the interest of national economy; this new business was operated from an office in Vyne Road, at the rear of the railway station.

By 1943 Basingstoke began to relax as air raids seemed to be a thing of the past. It was then revealed that the Germans had been dropping explosive objects across the countryside. A film was made about the dangers of picking these up, to be shown to schools and other establishments, but this did not deter some children from handling items they found. One boy, an evacuee, had his hand badly injured when he picked up an object at Kempshott village, while another lad had a shock when he threw a 'torch' that he had found, across the road where it exploded like a 'hand grenade'.

This spirit of adventure amongst local children led them to other impish antics during the war, especially as their fathers were away at the battle front. Static water tanks placed around the town, for the fire brigade to use during the war, became paddling pools for some youngsters, although the national fire service put up notices to warn them of the dangers of drowning. Fences were erected around the tanks, but at South Ham these were constantly pulled down. Even at school these mischievous youngsters were difficult to handle. At Fairfields, one lad was so disruptive that the teacher lost his temper and gave the boy such a thorough shaking that 'the scruffy kid dived out of the open window and ran off down the road'! During school dinners, pepper would be thrown about, making everyone sneeze; semolina ('not everyone's favourite') would be flicked across the table; and the table struts would sometimes be kicked away so that half the dinners would slide onto the floor.

Throughout the war, although almost everything was in short supply; the average person prevented a serious blaze. However, the most comical incident occurred when a postman, In addition to food rationing, milk, orange juice and cod liver oil were available to all the children. The youngsters were given a better diet than before the war, and also received better medical care. Even the suicide rate dropped to a third of what it was in the mid-1930s.

The presence of the military in and around the town gave local people a feeling of security, but a series of incidents in 1943 and 1944 were to raise questions as to whether the armed forces were safe. By the latter part of the war large numbers of American soldiers were based in Hampshire, some of whom were coloured, and at times there were brawls amongst the men. In May 1944 a group of white and coloured soldiers began to argue in Winchester Street and one of the Americans was shot in the leg. Within six months another shooting incident took place which nearly damaged the Anglo-American relationship. In October 1944 ten coloured American soldiers based at a camp near Kingsclere decided to have a drink at the *Crown Inn* in Kingsclere, but two U.S. military policemen ordered them back to the camp. They returned to their base, but, as the armoury was open, they helped themselves to guns and ammunition and went back to the public house, where they fired into the building and killed the military policemen and the landlady. The men were arrested and later found guilty in a court case at Thatcham, where they were sentenced to life imprisonment.

Another danger in the town came from speeding military vehicles, which caused several serious accidents. In November 1942 in London Road, three ladies who were waiting to cross the street were mown down by an army lorry, in a convoy, which lost control as it came out of Eastrop Lane. All three women were killed in the collision, which shook the town's folk to the extent that many protested at the way Basingstoke was being used by the military without any thought for road safety. In December 1944 an American army vehicle collided with a horse and cart in Winchester Street, and the cart was pushed into the window of Burton's outfitters. Fortunately no one was hurt, although the horse was somewhat shaken.

Through all the restrictions and bombing raids, the local folk looked for something to brighten their lives, and radio and cinema were two mediums that kept them smiling. The B.B.C. concentrated on radio comedy and variety shows to keep their listeners' morale high. Tommy Handley in I.T.M.A. (It's That Man Again), was a popular programme that began in the same month as the war. The weekly show soon attracted some 16 million listeners, with such characters as Colonel Chinstrap and Mrs. Mopp. Other shows included 'Bandwaggon' with Richard Murdoch and Arthur Askey; 'Happidrome' with the lovable characters Enoch, Ramsbottom and Mr. Lovejoy; and the general interest programme, 'Monday Night at Eight'. Shops, such as Currys in London Street, which sold electrical items, suddenly found that orders for radios exceeded the stock in their warehouse. With the closure of the television service, when war broke out, the radio was the only direct link with the news, although Fleet Street newspapers kept people well informed. The local newspaper, *The Hants and Berks Gazette*, based in Church Street, kept its readers in touch with events in and around Basingstoke and gave a brief outline of national news, especially concerning the war. The local cinemas, the Savoy, Waldorf, and Plaza, provided an assortment of films to entertain the crowds that swarmed there. Amongst the popular film stars was George Formby, the comedian, whose ukulele playing set people's toes tapping. In early 1944 the Gainsborough Film company arrived in Basingstoke with Formby to make the film *He Snoops to Conquer*, in which the town was renamed 'Tangleton'. The film concerned the corrupt workings of the town council who were doing nothing about post-war planning in the area. George Formby played the part of the Town Hall odd-job man who was supposed to destroy the letters of complaint concerning the lack of housing but instead he gets them blown about the town where they are seen by the locals who then eject the council members. Certain scenes were filmed in Church Square, where the bomb damage was still much in evidence. In another scene the set was besieged by dozens of school children from Brook Street School, at 'going home time', and the chatter of their voices was so obvious it almost drowned out George Formby's voice, much to the annoyance of the film director. While some of the film stars were staying at the *Red Lion Hotel*, in London Street, some of their property was stolen from their rooms. The police investigated the matter and traced the property to a private in the Royal Fusiliers, who was sentenced to nine months' imprisonment.

Throughout the war local firms contributed a great deal to the war effort especially Thornycrofts, who produced vehicles, guns and other equipment for the three services, including over 8,000 Bren gun carriers, nearly 700 sets of two-pounder guns, and a large assortment of other items. Thirteen thousand vehicles were also produced including mobile cranes, workshop lorries, and water carriers. One person who lived in Worting Road at the time remembers the constant rumbling and other noises coming from the factory as work went on all day and night to provide the necessary goods. At Kelvin's factory in Winchester Road various items were made for the Royal Air Force and Royal Navy, including altimeters, compasses, barometers, and other instruments for the two services' aircraft. The wear and tear on the roads in transporting the heavy vehicles to their destinations gave the local council plenty of work. It was decided that after the war a programme of road remaking would be one of the first items on the agenda.

The Normandy invasion in June 1944—known as D-Day—brought even more traffic onto the roads of Hampshire, with convoys of military vehicles heading towards the English Channel. Army camps, field hospitals, and supply depots were set up in the fields across the county, while a special petrol pipe-line, to supply the vehicles with fuel, was laid across Hampshire to the coast.

Within a year the allies had reached Germany and captured Berlin. VE Day—8 May 1945—brought an end to the war in Europe. Basingstoke heard the news over the radio, from Winston Churchill; then the mayor, Councillor Alfred Kirk, appeared on the Town Hall balcony to make a brief statement. Three hours later he reappeared to give a longer speech to the assembled crowd in the Market Square, in which he stated that celebrations could now take place in the town after six years of restrictions and hardships. The rest of the day saw the local folk rejoicing. Flags and bunting were pulled out from attics and cupboards and hung up in front of houses and shops in the town. Church bells were rung, and gramophones were wound up to play a medley of music for the people to dance and sing to in the streets. Trestle tables were laid out, food and cakes appeared, and the public houses supplied the drinks, and soon people were enjoying themselves eating, drinking, and making merry. There were games for the children to play, and some streets had parties for everyone to take part. Fairylights and floodlights were switched on to allow the celebrations to continue into the night.

The end of the war meant that work to repair the bomb damage in the town could begin, while tank blocks, built in 1939 to prevent German vehicles negotiating the local roads, were removed. Black-out material was taken from windows and thrown away, although some people found a use for it. One lady sent hers to the mountain villages of Greece for the village clergy to make into cassocks. In Basingstoke a Victory Parade was arranged and various local groups and organisations marched through the town to give thanks at St Michael's church for the end of the war. Over the following weeks there were farewell parties held by the various voluntary groups such as the Air Raid Wardens. But just when people thought that all their worries were over notices were issued warning that new ration books would be circulated due to a shortage of food and goods. It would be nearly another six years before all rationing ended.

1. A general view of Basingstoke just before the Second World War, looking west across the lower part of the town. The cluster of trees in the centre belonged to St Michael's church rectory grounds. Church Square, to the left, was to suffer bomb damage during the War.

2. The Electric Theatre in lower Wote Street before it became the Savoy Cinema in 1939. Swimming baths occupied the site before the Electric Theatre was built for showing films in 1910. The earliest films in Basingstoke were shown at the Corn Exchange in 1900 when a projector with a lamp of 3,000 candle power was used. The Electric brought crowds of people to the bottom of the town to see the shows and soon this part of Basingstoke became the mecca for entertainment.

3. Fairfields School before the Second World War. Built in 1886, this was a boarding school for both male and female senior pupils; a few yards further down the road was the juniors' school. The stone crowns on the roof, at either end of the building, were removed in 1939 as a precaution against bomb damage. The building can still be seen today.

4. In the 1930s South Ham Farm extended over a large area from Bramblys Grange to Buckskin Farm. By 1939 part of the land had been acquired for the council housing estate, and in the early 1950s further land was used for an extension to the estate. This 1938 view shows the farm as seen from Worting Road, with the long line of trees that now cover Peveral Walk. The farmland has since been built over and is now occupied by the South Ham housing estate.

5. Marks and Spencer's store in Winchester Street in 1936. Having acquired the old Burberry's warehouse in 1933 this modern building was opened the following year at a time when other multiple stores were also moving to Basingstoke. With some 15,000 people in the town and the prospect of the population increasing at a steady rate, commercial and retail trade in Basingstoke was also growing. Reproduced by permission of Marks & Spencer.

6. The architect's drawing of how the new Basingstoke hospital would have looked, after plans to acquire land in Cliddesden Road, just prior to the war, the funds for which would have come from annual fund-raising carnivals of that time. The outbreak of war prevented any further funds being raised, and the project was dropped. Money collected in that pre-war period went towards an out-patients department for the cottage hospital in Southern Road in 1956.

7. The Vyne Road cattle pens, at the rear of the railway station, before their removal to make way for a car park in the mid-1960s. It was here that many evacuated children from Southampton, Portsmouth, and other areas were herded in September 1939 to be given food and drink and to be informed where they were to be housed. The cattle market pens in front of the railway station were also used for this purpose. Some 900 children altogether were found homes in and around Basingstoke.

8. Park Prewett hospital in 1948, when Park Prewett Farm grew crops and vegetables on the surrounding land. During the war the large complex of buildings housed many of the men wounded in the conflict; the mental patients previously housed there had been moved elsewhere in the country.

9. Rooksdown House, near Park Prewett, where many of the burn victims of the Second World War were taken to be treated by a team of experts under the leadership of Sir Harold Gillies, the pioneer of plastic surgery. It was on these lawns that many of those victims rested in the sunny days of that time, when they were only too glad to be alive and happy that there was such an establishment where their burns and scars could be healed.

10. An early aerial photograph of Church Square before the bomb attack of 16 August 1940 altered the scene. Church Street runs through the picture, horizontally, with its various shops and offices.

11. The corner of Church Square where it joined Mortimer Lane, before the German air attack on 16 August 1940 when three bombs blasted the area. Church Lane was a foot-path with seven homes which lay between Church Square and Flaxfield Road. Also in the lane was the boot repair business of Mr. A. Jarvis.

12. The Thornycroft Civil Defence team of 1944, many of whom joined the voluntary force at the start of the war when it was realised that the large complex of buildings needed protection against any bomb or incendiary attacks. As elsewhere in the town, stirrup-pumps and buckets of water and sand were kept handy to put out any small fires. Thornycroft's was kept busy day and night in supplying vehicles for the war effort, and, because of this, it was an important military objective for the Germans. Fortunately it escaped any bomb attacks.

13. Known as Swiss Cottage, this hut-like building in Brook Street provided accommodation for most of the firemen who carried out auxiliary work during the Second World War. In the background can be seen the fire station which dated from 1913.

14. Even before Hitler sent his bombers to the cities and towns of Britain, booklets were issued to the public as a guide to protect their homes against air raids and the ravages of fire. These were two such booklets.

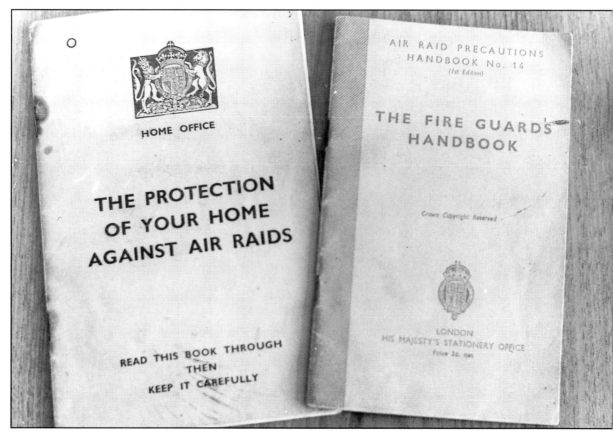

15. The view across Basingstoke from the top of the Plaza cinema, showing how prominent the Eli Lilly firm was. It was feared that German bombers would take their sightings from this 'beacon' as they flew in across Hampshire. The building was given a coat of camouflage paint in an attempt to prevent the German planes from seeing it.

16. A familiar sight visible for miles on the northern hill overlooking Basingstoke were the two mortuary chapels in the Holy Ghost Chapel cemetery. Erected in 1858 with spires 80 ft. high, they provided a place for prayer—one for Church of England members and the other for Non-conformists. Pictured in this photograph is the Non-conformist chapel. Both were pulled down, c.1955.

17. Essential items of the war years—ration books. Even after the war rationing continued, due to the shortage of certain goods and materials. Local shopkeepers soon looked upon the tearing out of coupons as a way of life, and when rationing ended in the early 1950s some of them were still looking for the ration books!

18. The Sarum Hill tank blocks, built to prevent German tanks manoeuvring into strategic positions should they ever reach Britain. Many local folk queried the position of these blocks, as they felt that they were not needed at this spot, as other areas around the town did not have them. Nevertheless these particular tank blocks stayed there until 1983.

19. The general scene in Church Square after the bomb attack on 16 August 1940. Taken from the top of the tower of St Michael's church, it shows how much damage was done by one of the bombs; six homes in Church Square and seven in Church Lane were hit.

20. The aftermath of the Church Square bombing raid, showing some of the damage to the buildings near Church Lane. It was close to here that an unexploded bomb blew up during the night after the raid, causing more damage and shaking the town centre.

21. Yet another scene of destruction in Church Square. Houses like this were made temporarily safe until complete demolition was possible. The area was levelled and remained like that until after the war, when memorial gardens and bungalows for the elderly were built.

22. The Church Street Methodist church after the Germans dropped several bombs in the Church Square area in August 1940. The frontage of the building was hardly damaged due to the strength of the stonework, but the blast of the bomb blew in the windows and badly damaged the organ at the rear of the church. The church was renovated after the war and re-opened in 1950.

23. St Michael's church, Church Square in 1954. The building was badly hit by the bombs which fell opposite in August 1940. With the completion of repair work after the roof fire of 1938, further restoration was again necessary to mend the windows and interior fittings which were damaged by the bomb blast.

24. The Roman Catholic chapel, seen here during the post-war years, was established in Sherborne Road in 1902. When the Germans attacked Basingstoke in August 1940 the chapel was badly shaken by the blast from the bomb that fell in Burgess Road, just along the road on which corner the chapel was built.

25. St Vincent's school in Cliddesden Road after a bomb landed by the side of it on 24 October 1940. Two women were killed as the blast devastated the building. The children from the private school were playing games in the nearby War Memorial Park and escaped injury. The houses on either side of the school were also damaged.

26. This photograph, c.1955, shows the site of the bomb attack on Bramblys Grange in November 1940. The electricity hut in the centre of the picture pin-points the spot where the bomb fell. The blast was mainly directed upward due to the soft ground, but some nearby houses were still badly damaged.

27. St Michael's church rectory, in Church Street, dates back to 1773. Although some of its windows were shattered by the bomb that fell in the grounds, in November 1940, no one was hurt by the blast. Shops and offices in the lower part of Church Street had their windows broken as well. (The building survived a serious fire in 1975, and was renamed Chute House. It is now used as offices for various voluntary groups, such as Age Concern.)

28. After the majority of the Church Square bomb-damaged buildings had been cleared up, a few wrecked houses remained on the Church Lane side. The cleared area was used for several years as an unofficial parking place until in the mid-1950s the land was turned into memorial gardens, and bungalows for the elderly.

29. During the war several people moved out of the town and lived in remote areas in case of bomb attacks. One such place was at Winklebury where temporary homes—in some cases, little more than huts and shacks—were built, and even a few railway carriages were drafted in. This photograph shows the type of terrain there in those days.

30. To escape the worries that war inevitably brings, many people visited the Black Dam ponds to stroll and study the wild life. There were four ponds altogether—Mill Head, Upper Fish and Lower Fish ponds and Black Dam itself. On the other side of the London Road were two more ponds belonging to the Upper Mill, used to grow watercress.

31. The Basingstoke Cottage hospital, on the corner of Southern Road and Hackwood Road, in pre-war days. During the Second World War many local bomb victims were treated here, or at the Park Prewett or Basing Road hospitals. Opened in 1879 the Cottage hospital relied on voluntary contributions until the National Health Service Act of 1946. (After the new hospital was built off the Aldermaston Road in the early 1970s the Cottage hospital was used as a psychiatric clinic. It was demolished in 1993.)

32. One item of great concern to people, whose property was damaged by air raids, was insurance. To replace essential furniture a lot of money was needed and the John Bull free air raid insurance attracted many people.

33. The demolition of the old British Restaurant buildings in lower Wote Street, 1962. Lord Woolton, Minister of Food (1883-1964) had the idea of providing self-service restaurants, run by local authorities to serve cheap meals for one shilling each (five pence now). The Basingstoke restaurant was opened in November 1942 and catered for hundreds of people during the Second World War, providing them with warm food as an incentive to work harder for the war effort. By the end of the war business at the restaurant was not so brisk and, having incurred a net loss of £282 during 1946, it closed in 1947.

34. Budd's Meadow in the early 1950s. This land, off Bramblys Grange Road, was to have a small estate of houses built on it some 20 years later. During the war the field was used for planting sugar beet and other vegetables, while at the top of the hill, on the Downsland private estate, there were blackberry bushes and apple trees which attracted children in the autumn.

35. During the war years a considerable number of grocery shops in the town were all hit by a shortage of supplies due to government restrictions. Some grocery shops were within yards of each other, such as this one in Essex Road belonging to J. W. Woodward, which stood close to the large co-operative stores in the background.

36. Street parties were soon arranged when news came through that the war in Europe was over. At Bramblys Grange benches were placed down the centre of the road as tables, and planks were placed on oil drums to provide seating. Food and drink was rustled up and entertainment in the form of games and music was provided by local folk.

37. Within weeks of the end of the war, work went ahead to remove most of the ugly tank blocks that had been put in strategic positions around the town. This one was outside Thornton's Bakery in Flaxfield Road and proved a tough obstacle due to its reinforced concrete.

Chapter Two

The Post-war Years, 1946-1955

As soon as the war in Europe ended, the decision was made to hold a General Election. Voting took place on 5 July 1945, and resulted in a landslide victory for the Labour Party, led by Mr. Clement Attlee. The new government immediately began a sweeping programme of economic and social reforms, which transformed Britain into the 'Welfare State'. Among the most important measures were the nationalisation of industries, such as electricity, transport, gas and iron and steel, and the establishment of the National Health Service, which provided free medical care for all.

When the electricity service came to be nationalised, a survey of the Basingstoke area revealed that several places were still not linked to the main supply, even though the Basingstoke generating station in Brook Street had been connected to the Central Electricity Board's system as far back as 1933. In the villages of Baughurst, Tadley and Pamber Heath, the electricity supply was non-existent as the Air Ministry prevented the siting of electricity poles close to the Aldermaston Aerodrome, as they were considered a hazard to aircraft. Patrick Donner, the M.P. for Basingstoke, approached the ministry about the matter, and in 1948 he persuaded them to allow the electricity board to supply the area with that essential service.

Another feature of the post-war period was the need for housing, as six years had passed with no house building for the growing population. In the case of Basingstoke there had been an increase of nearly one thousand people during the war years, and it was evident that new homes were needed as soon as possible. The government decided to help by introducing prefabricated units, which could be assembled swiftly and came complete with all home comforts. The first 'prefabs' were erected in Sandys Road on the South Ham estate in June 1945, and more were built in the following months. In each prefab, there were seven rooms: a hall, living-room, kitchen, two bedrooms, bathroom and a toilet. Also included were a dozen cupboards, fuel and 'pram' sheds, and a medium-sized garden. The living-room measured 14½ ft. by 10½ ft., while the walls were nearly two inches thick and fully insulated for heat. As soon as building materials were available, the local council set about building homes of the more traditional type, such as those at Southview and South Ham.

The National Health Service brought an influx of people into the doctors' surgeries in Basingstoke, which caused 'several headaches in ordering medicines' at the various chemists in the town. Most people wanted their free supply of medication whilst others were delighted to have spectacles and dental treatment without having to pay. By the end of 1948, when the National Health Scheme came into being, the nation's health was set to improve considerably.

Soon after the war, the B.B.C. restarted its television service, and during the following years the local electrical shops began to sell the latest television sets, although the transmission from London was far from perfect. To make matters worse, interference from the ignition systems of motor vehicles and other equipment affected the television picture to such an extent that new rules and regulations concerning the fitting of suppressors were introduced by the government. As far as Watson's Garage in Wote Street was concerned, this brought in a great deal of trade. Several drivers turned up in cars from the 1920s and '30s, as no new cars had been manufactured in the war. Most of the factories had been taken over for the construction of military vehicles, and it took a few years for the factories to get back to normal production. The steady increase in traffic would eventually bring the town to a halt, so one-way roads were planned to keep the traffic moving. In 1952 the first traffic lights were installed where Church Street met Brook Street and Chapel Street.

After the return to peace-time activities, local sporting organisations looked forward to better times, and both time and money were spent to attract more spectators. During the war clubs had to close down, one being Basingstoke Football Club. After a special meeting in August 1945 it was agreed that the first Hants League match should be against Andover at Castle Field, near Fairfields School, on 15 September that year. Basingstoke played well but were beaten 2—1, although further games proved more successful. After several matches at Castle Field the club was informed that an alternative ground would have to be found, and at one stage it looked as if it might have to be disbanded. Then Lord Camrose of Hackwood Park, who owned land in the area, came to their rescue with the offer of a long lease on land in Winchester Road. Although the land had a distinct slope on, it was eventually levelled and dressing-rooms and a stand were built. Over the following years the Basingstoke club became one of the best in the Southern League.

The Cricket Club at May's Bounty had been able to keep going through the war, but even they decided to make improvements. The pavilion was not in the best of condition and the score-board was replaced in 1949, and funds were sought for extending and modernising the pavilion.

The Golf Club, at Kempshott, having been reduced to nine holes during the war (the other part had been used for grazing purposes), was soon restored to 18 holes and by 1948 its membership was on the increase. Over the following years famous golfers were invited to compete in the championship games which attracted more attention to the club, and its attractive parkland and 200–year-old beech trees. In the late 1940s the sporting scene in Basingstoke saw the establishment of many clubs, such as Basingstoke Hockey Club, Waverley Badminton Club, and Basingstoke Rugby Club. By 1950 there had been a tremendous growth of interest in cycling. Basingstoke had its own club based in a large hut in Winchester Road, near Bramblys Grange, from where all sorts of activities took place, including hill climbs and time trials, which were held out in the countryside, some over distances of 50 miles. The boxing scene saw many local men such as Jack Gardner, Don Cockell, Vince Hawkins, and Freddie Simpson rise to fame in tournaments held at places such as the Thornycroft Canteen. Jack Gardner, who weighed 16 stone and was over six feet tall in his bare feet, won the British, Empire and European heavyweight titles during the following year, while Vince Hawkins became the British Middleweight champion. This awareness of sport brought about the opening of the Thornycroft Sports Ground on the West Ham estate in 1948, where cricket, bowls, and other games could be played.

As the country slowly returned to normal in those post-war years so the economic situation improved, although with the return of servicemen the unemployment figures began to rise. For Basingstoke this problem hardly arose as the town council had made plans. They bought land from Merton Farm, along the Kingsclere Road, and advertised it for sale for industrial purposes. In 1949 the industrial truck manufacturer, Lansing Bagnall, acquired a large area of the land for its present complex of buildings for the production of vehicles and equipment, including its world famous fork-lift truck. In the meantime Thornycroft's factory was also increasing its range of goods, having been released from its obligation to the government at the end of the war. In 1951 another newcomer to the local scene was Van Moppes factory in Lister Road, off Winchester Road, which specialised in making diamond tools for a variety of reasons, including boring and grinding. Within a few years, as production increased, further extensions were built in 1954.

At the end of January 1947, severe wintry conditions set in across the country. Snowstorms brought the railways and roads to a halt, while blizzards stopped ships sailing around the coast. This brought chaos, especially in coal transportation, which was essential for the power stations supplying the country with electricity. On 7 February, Mr. Shinwell, the Minister of fuel and power, told the Houses of Parliament that coal stocks were very low at power stations and action would have to be taken to prevent a complete power breakdown. A month of power cuts followed and two million people in Britain found themselves temporarily out of work. In Basingstoke the heavy snow blocked some main roads, especially the Kingsclere Road, while the icy conditions brought the town centre almost to a halt. The Joint Nurseries, off the Winchester Road, recorded 29 degrees fahrenheit of frost at times, while blizzards stopped the Town Hall clock. By April the cold weather had abated and the town returned to normal, although massive road repairs had to be carried out because of the intense cold and frost.

Shortly after the end of the war the 'ill wind' of the conflict began to benefit the country with its stimulation of inventions and discoveries. New ideas in science and industry brought about a mass of goods designed to make people's lives more comfortable, and by the 1950s these were prominent in shops and stores all over the world. For Basingstoke shopkeepers this vast range of new goods increased their sales areas. Builders found that the 'Do-it-yourself' movement, which started just after the war, was taking trade away from them. At Sapp's offices in Hackwood Road people began to ask for building materials instead of asking the workmen to do the work for them. Brightening up homes after the drabness of the war involved redecorating and rebuilding, so naturally people did not want to spend too much money on the work. An army of amateur builders and decorators soon came onto the scene (some with no experience), while many householders did the work themselves, a trend which has continued ever since.

The most important event which affected the design of mass-produced goods in this country was the Festival of Britain, a large exhibition on the South Bank of the River Thames in London in 1951. It attracted manufacturers and buyers from all over the world, and for five months over eight million people visited this show of British goods and design.

'Change' seemed to be the key note of the early 1950s, although some business people had already brought modernisation to certain goods. The 'New Look', promoted mainly by the French designer Christian Dior in 1947, brought a reaction against the austere and restricted wartime styles, and allowed women to wear dresses that were more stylish and feminine. Men's clothes were mainly influenced by American fashions, and the younger generation in Britain were soon wearing colourful and loose-fitting jackets and trousers. Local clothing shops and outfitters realised that a new trend was 'hitting the market', so they began to reduce their stock of suits and other formal wear and ordered the more modern clothing.

Festival Year saw a brighter Basingstoke, with the restoration of many buildings damaged during the war, while plans were drawn up to restore Church Square. One local man suggested that it should become a War Memorial Garden, and this materialised into the present site, which was completed in 1955.

The Festival Year was a good opportunity to hold a carnival week in Basingstoke, similar to those held before the war. The borough council asked Brian Edney, the furniture store owner in Winton Square, to form a committee and soon a group of local businessmen organised a highly successful week of events, funds from which went towards restoring Deane's Almshouses in London Street. A carnival queen was selected—Miss Derrie Brennam—and many local firms took part in the colourful procession on the Thursday of that week.

Those garish days were epitomised by the lavish life-style of Lord and Lady Docker, who travelled around in a gold Daimler. They came to Basingstoke in June 1955 to attend the County Archery Championships in West Ham Park. As the wealthy chairman of the Daimler company, Sir Bernard Docker was a keen yachtsman and golfer. Born in 1897 and knighted in 1939, he married Norah, widow of Sir William Collins, in 1949. The event at Basingstoke gave many local people the opportunity to see this couple close-up and to admire their large and luxurious car.

Local people worked hard to reconstruct the Church Street Methodist church, which had been so badly damaged by the bomb which fell in front of it in August 1940. The Ministry of Works finally allowed the church to be rebuilt, and on 7 September 1950 it was reopened by the mayor and mayoress. Work had also been allowed on St Michael's church, where shrapnel had caused many scars to its walls and had blown out most of its windows. For many years after the war a sizeable congregation still attended local churches to give thanks that peace had come, but by the early 1950s there was a distinct sign that attendances were declining. The pre-war habits of the sabbath, such as family prayers and Sunday observance, slowly disappeared, although many people still continued to believe in Christianity.

As soon as supplies of paper began to arrive from Canadian mills, and from other sources which had been stopped during the war, local people revived their interest in the printer's word. Many joined the private libraries in the town, such as at Boot's the Chemists, the Chain library in Church Street, and the smaller ones such as at the tobacconist's of Mrs. Kemp at Flaxfield Road.

In the early 1950s people's leisure time extended to the theatre, which had seen many changes not only in its management but also in the type of performances. The local council carried out repairs and decoration to the Grand Theatre, which was then renamed the Haymarket. Various groups, such as the Phoenix Players, used the theatre for their shows, and this gave a new lease of life. Another group, the Thornycroft and Basingstoke Amateur Operatic Society, provided the town with an annual performance of Gilbert and Sullivan's operettas, which proved very popular. Many people came from places as far as Surrey and Berkshire to see these shows.

In April 1950 construction began on the Atomic Weapons Research Establishment at Aldermaston, and accommodation for the staff was built at Tadley and Basingstoke, the latter on land which belonged to Oakridge Farm to the north of the town. The disused aerodrome at Aldermaston was converted into accommodation, canteen and office areas for the construction workers, which numbered up to 4,000 at one time. Over the following months the specialised processing buildings designed for the investigation and manufacture of components in plutonium and conventional high explosives were built. Dr. William

Penney, who was director of the huge complex of buildings, lived in a detached house on the outskirts of the site. He was already well known for his research work on nuclear weapons, and was an observer when the atomic bomb was dropped on Nagasaki.

Education in Basingstoke saw many changes in the decade after the war, including the construction of new schools. In 1950 the Shrubbery and Charles Chute schools were built at either ends of the town, the former in Cliddesden Road and the latter in Queen Mary's Avenue. In 1948, after 60 years of separate departments, the boys' and girls' schools at Fairfields were amalgamated. No more would there be a ban on either sex going upstairs or downstairs to the 'wrong' department. And the school-leaving age was raised to 15 in 1947, some 11 years after the Baldwin administration had agreed to the move. The war had caused the suspension of the Act, the original date being 1 September 1939—two days before the outbreak of war.

38. Lower Wote Street, *c.*1948, with the Venture bus station on the right. In the top left hand corner is Wallis and Steevens factory which was started by Mr. Wallis in 1860 as a small business in the market place. This part of Basingstoke was once known as the Soke, while the area around the Town Hall was called the Upland. In the 19th century Soke and Upland were names used by the locals as a means of differentiating between 'them' and 'us'.

39. Basingstoke Common was enjoyed by the locals before the land was acquired by a compulsory purchase order issued by Basingstoke Council on 12 July 1969. In the background are the trees of the Black Dam wild life area, to which many people walked on a Sunday afternoon, to feed the swans and other aquatic creatures.

40. Part of Southview housing estate, which was started in 1946. This council estate was the first attempt to house the ever increasing population of Basingstoke, some houses being made of pre-cast reinforced concrete. In the background is the Oakridge tower, which was built in 1967.

41. New Road in the late 1940s, showing one of the few car parking places in the town. In 1937 Brinkletts Farm in Winchester Road was cleared and made into a car park, but the increase in traffic led to more calls for parking facilities. Eventually the land to the rear of London Street and New Road was acquired for the central car park and was completed in January 1957.

42. Kelvin, Bottomley and Baird soon established itself in the sporting life of the town with its football and cricket teams, and a first-class bowling green where many championships took place. The large sports field gave the staff the opportunity to unwind and relax during the war years, when the factory was working day and night to produce aeroplane instruments and other equipment. In recent years the bowling green and sports field has become disused.

43. Basingstoke Football Club in 1949, in front of the changing hut in Winchester Road. Told that they could no longer use the Castle Field pitch for their weekly matches, Lord Camrose came to their aid and gave them part of his land in Winchester Road.

44. With the end of the Second World War, the annual Remembrance Day ceremony in November became the focus of the town's attention. In this view, c.1955, the locals are gathered in the War Memorial Park to offer prayers and to remember those who died to give us peace.

45. May's Brewery in Brook Street. It was established in 1755 by the May family but was taken over in 1920 when John May died. This large complex of buildings saw nearly 200 years of beer making before it was closed down in 1950. After the death of Edward Blatch, the director of the brewery, in 1946, negotiations went ahead for the sale of the business to a Maidenhead firm, but they sold it to Simonds of Reading, who then closed it three years later. The building was demolished during the latter part of 1966 and early 1967.

46. Listening to the band in the War Memorial Park in the 1950s. For many people Sunday in the summer was never complete without a stroll to the park to enjoy the music played on the bandstand by various local bands. Not far away were the bowling green and tennis courts.

IN AID OF THE ST. JOHN AMBULANCE BRIGADE
(BASINGSTOKE and DISTRICT DIVISION)

GRAND

Under the Licence of the B.B.B. of C.

BOXING!

TOURNAMENT

At Messrs.
THORNYCROFT
CANTEEN
WORTING ROAD
BASINGSTOKE

By Kind Permission of
Transport Equipment Thornycroft Ltd.
PROMOTERS: B. Thornton, Esq. and F. Draper, Esq.
Referee Appointed by B.B.B. of C.

SATURDAY
NOV. 27TH
1948

Doors open at 6.30 p.m.
Commence at 7.30 p.m.

Great Special Six 3 min. Rounds Contest at 9st. 6lbs.

IVOR   JIMMY
SIMPSON v. SHOORD

BASINGSTOKE. Now matched to box Al Bessell for No. 2 Southern   BETHNAL GREEN. Ex Lightweight Champion of the Royal
Area Featherweight Championship. Simpson has k.o. wins over Roy   Navy. Beaten Charlie Wisdom, Paddy Judge, took Harry
Coles, Danny Nagle, Tony Bazil, Tommy Davis, etc.   McMurdie to close verdict at the Royal Albert Hall.

Grand Six 3 min. Rounds Contest at 10st. 7lbs.

FREDDIE WHEELER v. RON JONES

BASINGSTOKE. Always game for money. Winner of over 100 contests.   COWES. Now matched to box Frank McAvoy for
Beaten Harry Legg, Frank McAvoy, etc.   No. 2 Area Welterweight Championship.

Sensational Six 3 min. Rounds Contest at 12st. 7lbs.

TREVOR LOWDER v. JOE ROMERO

BASINGSTOKE.   Two whole-hearted fighters to provide thrills.   JAMAICA.

Great Special Attraction : 3 Rounds Exhibition Contest

JACK   DON
GARDNER v. COCKELL

LEICESTER. British Amateur Heavyweight Champion, 1948, Army and   BATTERSEA. The brilliant young Lightheavyweight and K.O. King.
I.S.B.A. Champion, 1948, British Olympic Representative, 1948. Makes his   Winner of over 40 contests against the very best, a future champion
pro. debut in Jack Solomon's £1000 competition at Harringay on Dec. 6th.   and winner of the "Star" Trophy, Wembley, 1942.

Grand Return Six 3 min. Rounds Contest at 9st.

JOHNNIE FRENCH v. BILLY BURNELL

EASTLEIGH.   This is sure to be a great slam.   BRISTOL.

Special Four Rounds Contest at 9st.

JEFF HOLDSWORTH v. BENNY BURR

SLOUGH   CROYDON

ADMISSION (INCLUDING TAX)—

TICKETS: £1:1:0   No. and Reserved   10/6   No. and Reserved   5/-   Reserved   3/6

47. One of the many posters printed in the late 1940s to advertise boxing tournaments at Thornycroft's Canteen in Worting Road. Boxing stars such as Jack Gardner and Don Cockell attracted people from afar, while some of the local pugilists also gave good performances.

48. Buckskin Farm at Kempshott before any local development. In the distance is the village of Kempshott, with Pack Lane joining Buckskin Lane and Kempshott Lane at the point called Fiveways. It was here that horse-racing took place every year from the early 19th century until 1859.

49. The bleak scene at South View during one of the many blizzards of 1947, when the great Freeze-up kept most people indoors for weeks. As the extreme cold and heavy snow continued from late January to April, so all transport came to a halt, and fuel cuts led to people shivering in their houses, and offices and shops closed down for short periods.

50. As soon as the war ended, local folk were able to get back to normal, and the cinemas and theatres found that business was good. With street lighting and other services improving, more people went out at night to enjoy themselves. Programmes such as these were printed to advertise future films and shows.

51. Basingstoke Museum, on the top floor of the old Mechanics' Institute in New Street in the post-war years. Established in 1931, the museum was acquired by Hampshire County Council some 20 years later, with George Willis, one of the three men who helped to assemble the many exhibits, as curator. His name is used in the title of the present museum, which is now at the old Town Hall.

52. The crossroads at Essex Road, Penrith Road and Worting Road in the 1950s, with the prominent Essex Lodge house. Traffic lights were erected here in April 1967 to prevent road accidents, although within a few years Essex Road was closed at its east end, after the ring road roundabout was constructed. Essex Lodge was demolished, c.1980, and an office block was built on the site.

53. The decorations outside the Town Hall for the Queen's Coronation in 1953. Unfortunately the weather proved rather damp for outdoor celebrations, but the local folk still enjoyed themselves with indoor parties and dinners.

54. Upper Wote Street in the early 1950s. In the background is the Town Hall with its clock tower. On the right is the Haymarket Theatre, which prior to 1951 was known as the Grand Theatre. It was here that many famous names from stage and screen appeared in their early days, often staying at the *Royal Exchange* (on the left). During the war people such as 'Gert' and 'Daisy' and other radio stars kept the local folk laughing.

55. On point duty in the Market Place in the early 1950s, a police officer prepares to hand over his white gloves to his replacement. Behind them is Kingdon's hardwear store, whilst on the corner is Timothy White's and Taylor's shop. *The George Hotel* was established in the 16th century, but rebuilt in 1819.

56. The Tadley Wolf Cub group assembling with other local organisations for the Basingstoke Mayor's Parade in 1955, in the Market Place. In the background, between *The George Hotel* and the International general food stores, is the hardware shop of Thomas Kingdon, the main supplier of garden and house tools in the town. As with Punter's in Wote Street it was to capitalise on the D.I.Y. craze of the 1960s.

57. The White Garage in Winchester Road during alterations, *c*.1955. Mackies', the cleaners, was taken over to extend the business, while offices were built above the garage. Problems arose because the petrol pump pipes tripped people as cars were being refuelled at the roadside.

58. Cleaning the streets of Basingstoke in the 1950s. This scene shows Winchester Street in the early hours of a summer morning. The window sun-blinds were left down all night in readiness for the sun's appearance the following morning.

59. This illustration shows how busy Basingstoke was on Saturdays in the mid-1950s before the central car park was opened off New Road. With traffic on both sides of the road in lower Church Street, the motorist found it difficult to find anywhere to park.

60. New Road in the early 1950s. This scene, near the London Street crossroads, was a quiet area at one time, with very little traffic. Now that the road has been widened, it is one of the busiest roads in the town after the pedestrianisation of London Street in 1976 and the town centre in 1988.

61. Curry's electrical shop in London Street in the early 1950s, when they sold an assortment of goods, including bicycles and prams. The site of the shop was an old inn, *The Fleur de Lys*, which was pulled down in 1870. It was here that Oliver Cromwell stayed at times in the 17th-century Civil War, during the siege of Basing House to the east of Basingstoke.

62. *The Engineer's Arms* public house, on the corner of Reading Road and Basing Road in the 1950s. It became the popular drinking house of the workmen from Wallis and Steeven's factory, which was just across the road. The junction was the scene of many road accidents and in *c*.1965 part of the pub's side wall was knocked down.

63. Winchester Street in the 1950s, when traffic was at a minimum. Taken on a Sunday morning, the photograph shows how deserted the town centre was in the days before Sunday trading. Joice's Motor Coach Works had originally produced horse carriages, then changed to motor coach manufacture. Business ceased in 1950 and the buildings were damaged by fire in May 1960 and then in April and October 1964. Arnold Joice died in September 1969.

64. Advertising Speeds Wool Shop, London Street, in 1955, with Mrs. White the manageress standing on the right. Using an old pre-war car with a banner attached was a novel way of attracting customers who may have been unaware of the small business which opened almost opposite the *Red Lion Hotel*.
(It was to close down in December 1993.)

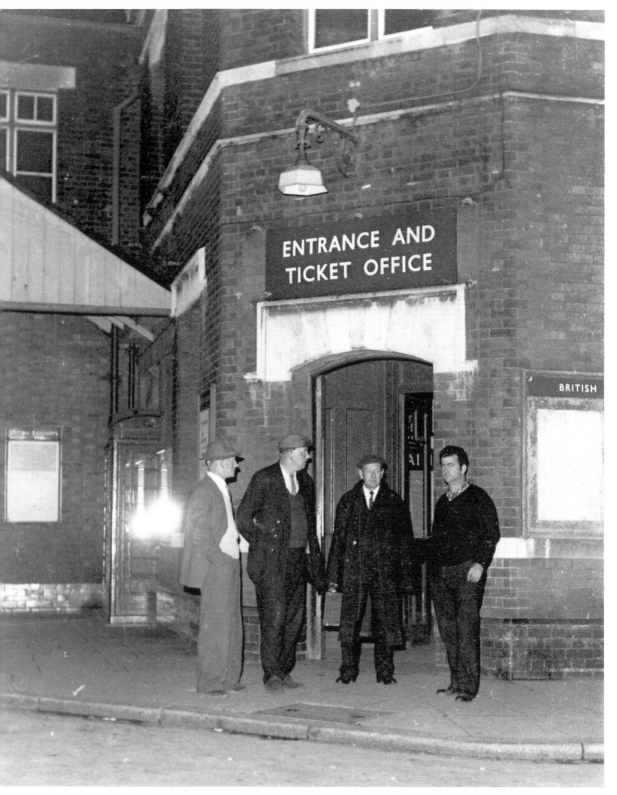

65. At midnight on 28 May 1955 the doors of the railway station at Basingstoke were closed for the first time in years. This was due to a railway strike by the railway union, A.S.L.E.F., which lasted for 17 days. A State of Emergency was declared by Parliament on 31 May, and many goods, including the mail, had to be transported by road. On 14 June the strike was called off, the dispute, about wages, finally being resolved after much discussion.

66. Reading Road Salvation Army headquarters in the mid-1950s. On its arrival in the town in 1880, it was first based at an old silk mill in Brook Street before moving to this new building. It was demolished in the 1960s to make way for the Town Development Scheme. A new headquarters was built at Wessex Close, off Winchester Road.

67. When Bramblys Grange private houses were built in 1939, off Winchester Road, some of the houses in the close were left unfinished due to the outbreak of war. Also not completed was the steep road up to the Winchester Road, and in winter this became a hazardous track. Finally, in 1955, contractors set about laying a proper surface for vehicles to get to the health centre, newly established in the old mansion house.

68. The Basingstoke Co-operative Society furnishing store, at the top of Sarum Hill, shortly after its opening in 1955. The building was originally a drill hall built in 1883, but in 1925 it became the Pavilion and was used as a dance hall. In 1931 it was turned into the Plaza Cinema, which eventually closed down in 1954. (The building was demolished in 1981—just two years short of its centenary.) The site now houses an office block, occupied by S. M. S., an American firm supplying computer software to hospitals and clinics.

69. In 1951 the Wilts and Dorset bus company took over the local bus service and acquired their offices and depot as well. The photograph shows one of the buses and its conductor at the Victoria Street depot, where most of the buses were kept under cover. Built in 1926 for the Venture Bus company, this building was pulled down in the late 1960s to make way for the new road system.

70. Church Street at the junction with Cross Street in 1955. The Warren shop was one of the most popular in the town. The hive of activity resulted from people coming from the New Street post office down Cross Street and into Church Street to reach Potters Lane and Wote Street.

71. Long before the town was developed in the 1960s, Basingstoke had a large area of farmland to the west. This photograph shows the fields that made up South Ham and Buckskin farms. The foreground now contains the Berg private housing estate and the background the Buckskin council estate.

72. The semaphore signals to the west of the Basingstoke railway station. These were replaced, c.1967, by the present-day signalling system after electrification of the line. Taken in 1955, this photograph shows part of the old sheds where repairs were carried out.

73. *The New Inn*, at Sarum Hill, opposite the Flaxfield post office, in the mid-1950s. More recently the yard at the rear has been altered to allow an extension to the building, while the houses further back have been demolished to make way for homes for the elderly. The area was often flooded during the winter months by the River Loddon.

74. Kelvin Hill, on the South Ham estate, during its construction in 1953/4. Some of the houses were built of pre-cast reinforced concrete, which in later years were found to be affected by damp penetration. Although most were found to be structurally sound, the local council is in the process of deciding whether to demolish or repair them. This decision also affects other houses of the same nature in the town.

75. The South Ham housing estate in 1954, shortly after its construction. The photograph shows Hillview Road looking down on the fields of Winchester Road, now the site of the Lister Road factories.

76. The Kings Road shops, on the South Ham estate, during the early 1950s. This area was undergoing a great deal of change at the time, with the fields of South Ham Farm slowly being built on. The field in the foreground of this picture now contains Kings Road Flats, which have recently been renovated.

77. Western Way in the mid-1950s when the South Ham housing estate was under construction. The Richard Aldworth school had yet to be built on the land in the background (left). In the distance the Roman Catholic church and hall of St Joseph's can be seen. It was built in the late 1950s and held its first mass in September 1959. It was replaced by the new St Joseph's in St Michael's Road in 1988. The Western Way Hall was demolished and houses were built on the site.

78. Unloading pigs at the Basingstoke Cattle Market. Established in 1873 by the Raynbird family on land close to the railway station, the market was held every Wednesday and brought farmers from all over Hampshire and Berkshire to buy and sell their cattle and other animals.

79. Local farmers gaze at the cows just herded into the Cattle Market ring in the 1950s. The Cattle Market, close to the railway station, was established after the success of fat stock sales and monthly cattle markets. Cattle were herded down Station Hill to the slaughter-house in Wote Street after being sold, and traffic often came to a halt as sheep and cows blocked the road. The Cattle Market came to an end in May 1966 after the site was acquired for Town Development.

80. The Basingstoke G.P.O. sorting office in the 1950s during the week before Christmas, when relief staff helped the postmen to sort out the mail, a practice not carried out any more. As can be seen in the photograph, the ages varied from teenagers to old-age pensioners. The atmosphere was always cheerful whatever the time of day, and by Christmas Eve a selection of seasonal fare would be produced, such as mince-pies, for all to enjoy. In those days postmen delivered mail on Christmas Day.

81. Some of the telephonists at the New Street telephone exchange in the early 1950s, when manual work was carried out. Under the scrutiny of a supervisor, the exchange was operated by a team of men and women throughout the day and night. With the introduction of S.T.D. in the late 1960s this type of exchange was phased out.

82. Mr. Malcolm Bell delivering parcels in the town centre in the 1950s. The post office found that the easiest way to deliver mail around the busy streets of Basingstoke was by this wicker hand cart. Within a few years it was ousted by the post office van.

83. In the 1950s many publicans in Basingstoke began to redesign their public houses and to install music boxes to attract customers. One public house, the *Horse & Jockey*, had an electric organ and held music evenings and other forms of entertainment. After a while it became difficult to find a quiet, old-fashioned beer-house. One public house, established in the 17th century, which did keep its antiquity was *The Self Defence* in Church Street. It was demolished in 1966 to make way for town development.

84. Preparing for the start of the 'Round the houses' race in Hill View Road, an annual event which was held on the South Ham housing estate in the 1950s and '60s. In the background are the Kings Road shops and flats built in 1953.

85. The annual rectory garden parties, held in lower Church Street, were well attended throughout the war years and beyond. Started in 1905 by the local vicar, Rev. H. Boustead, the event was the venue for many of the local people in those early years, and by the 1960s a large number of stalls and variety acts kept the folk entertained. In 1970 the rectory and its grounds were acquired by the local council and the garden parties came to an end. The photograph shows a gymnastic display in 1956 organised by Wilf Stocker, a local sportsman.

Chapter Three
Prelude to Development, 1956-1965

In 1944 the Greater London Plan was published providing for one million people to be dispersed from the London area to regions as far away as Hampshire and Hertfordshire. Among the various towns suggested for 'overspill' was Basingstoke, and when the Town Development Act of 1952 was passed by parliament it was listed as one of many that could relieve the congestion in the over-populated city of London. Hook village, near Basingstoke, was thought to be an ideal site for a 'new town', and in 1961 a book was produced stating the benefits of having a community in that area of Hampshire.

However, after a great deal of preliminary work, the Hampshire County Council decided on major town expansion schemes at Andover, Tadley and Basingstoke. The Hook scheme was dropped due to the outcry by local people, especially certain dignitaries. In October 1961, the Hampshire County Council, London County Council and Basingstoke Borough Council signed an agreement to expand Basingstoke with overspill from the London area.

For many people, town planning was a completely new concept, but the order and arrangement of streets in towns goes back to ancient times. By the Middle Ages most of the towns and cities in this country had become a jumbled mass of buildings, and it was not until the end of the 19th century that local authorities in Britain began to lay down rules and regulations on the construction of buildings. Eventually the Town Planning Act of 1909 enforced local authorities to control the development of their towns, while the 1925 Act gave them the power to control future expansion.

In 1940 the Pears Soap advertisements put forward their ideas for the future, in which residential districts would be designed on the garden city principle of villas or semi-detached houses, each with its own garden. Schools and playgrounds for children would be included, while the shopping centre would have special arcades for all-year-round cover.

The main local news in 1956 concerned the fire at the municipal buildings in March, when the upper floor was badly damaged, and many old documents were destroyed. Another fire, two months before, gutted Kelvin and Hughes sports pavilion, just one year after it had been opened. In August the town was horrified to hear of the murder of a patient at Park Prewett mental home. Two student male nurses were quickly charged with the killing and the case was soon forgotten, but within 18 months, in January 1958, another murder shook the town. A teenage girl was strangled by her boyfriend near the West Ham waterworks. One year later a murder in a house in New Road, Basingstoke, became famous because the murder trial was the shortest on record. The accused man pleaded guilty and was sentenced to life imprisonment, the whole procedure lasting just thirty seconds.

In 1957 a house on the Southview housing estate was the focus of media attention when poltergeist visitations caused a disturbance. The following year the same thing happened, but after a while the trouble faded away. The occupants survived the ordeal although it was frightening at the time, and no explanation was ever found.

Another important event was the opening of the new bus station on the site of the old canal wharf in lower Wote Street in June 1962. The Mayor of Basingstoke, Councillor John Peat, formally opened the station by cutting a tape to allow the first double-decker bus to enter. Designed to handle some 180,000 departures a year the station covered an area of 6½ acres. The bus company, the Wilts and Dorset, had acquired the local bus service, the Red and White, in 1951. Previously the Venture company had been the local service.

In July 1960 the main roads in the town centre were turned into one-way streets, to allow traffic to flow more easily. Until then a great deal of concern had been expressed about the chaos caused by the increase in road vehicles. Winchester Street and London Street traffic had to flow from west to east while diverted vehicles passed through Southern Road and down Victoria Street. In the same year it was announced that the M3 motorway was to be built south of the town.

From 1960 onwards it seemed to local folk that the town was slowly being altered and many familiar sights were disappearing. The west side of New Street had been demolished to make way for a large co-operative store, and in 1961 the Town Hall clock tower was removed and the Winchester Road Alton Light Railway bridge was demolished. In Pack Kempshott, the tall trees that had lined the road for over a hundred years were found to be diseased, and many of them were cut down. At the Conservative Club in Church Street, £5,000 worth of alterations were carried out to improve the facilities for its 400 members, who were unaware that within a few years the club would be demolished.

It was only after the signing of the Town Development Scheme that most local people became aware of the drastic changes that were about to take place in Basingstoke. There had been talk for many years that the town could face an increase in population from the London area, but in what form no-one knew, except those 'at the top'. The agreement resulted in the demolition of the town centre and the construction of a new shopping area and multi-storey car park. In addition a new road system was to be introduced, 8,000 houses were to be built, together with industrial and commercial sites around the town. This mammoth task meant that most of the services, such as gas, water, and electrical mains, had to be renewed completely. Roads had to be closed and rebuilt, bus routes altered, and even the River Loddon, which flowed through the lower part of town, was to be diverted. In August 1962 the proposals for the development of the town were put on display at the Town Hall, and meetings were held to allow the public to discuss the alterations. What concerned people, whose homes were due for demolition, was the amount of compensation and where they were going to live. This was taken care of in the agreement, whereby a proportion of the houses built in the town would be used for the many people whose homes were to be demolished. Unfortunately this did not include shopkeepers and other businessmen who were to lose their buildings in the development of the town centre. There were few places for them to move to, except to some shop units in an area which became the New Market Place, near the bus station. Many of the small shops which were forced to close never re-opened. Many shopkeepers found that their compensation was too small to re-start their businesses elsewhere.

By 1963 the construction of housing estates for the people from London was under way, and soon the fields around Basingstoke were the scene of much activity. At South Ham Farm, which only 10 years earlier had seen an extension to the old housing estate, another area was taken over to build yet more homes. It was to stretch across to the Buckskin Farm, which in turn was also to be built upon. At Winklebury, where many folk had been living in shanty homes, where the tracks were so rough that very few vehicles attempted to enter the area, another large estate was built. At the nearby private Clarke estate residents protested about the high density of development at Winklebury; while people living in Eastfield Avenue and Lytton Road, off London Road, in 1964, were concerned about the size of the Riverdene housing estate. The contractors of this latter estate were to cause further upset when they cut down several of the fine tall trees which had lined the avenue along London Road for over a hundred years.

By July 1964 the one thousandth family housed under the Town Development Scheme had moved into its home. Only the month before, a married couple and their 10 children had been moved to Basingstoke, from London, into two houses that were converted into one home.

All this meant a sudden increase in population from 25,980 in 1961 to 33,000 by 1965. Facilities in the town would have to be improved, and over the following years various local establishments were re-housed or enlarged. Doctors' surgeries were built, new schools erected, extra old people's homes constructed, and new nursery services provided.

After the success of the pre-war carnivals and the festival year celebrations, it was decided to form an annual carnival committee from 1956. The suggestion, made by a member of the Royal Air Force Association, was to raise money for a community centre, but other people and societies also joined in. The first carnival, in 1956, raised £677 and by 1959 £4,000 had been collected. By 1964 there was enough money, helped by a grant from a local authority, to start work on the centre, which was built in Council Road. Carnival queens were selected each year along with their attendants, the first one being Miss Jean Noyce of London Road, Basing. Each day of carnival week was devoted to a different event: Saturday afternoon was the opening ceremony and the crowning of the queen; Monday was Mardi Gras night, with dancing in the market place and nearby streets; Tuesday saw athletics in the War Memorial Park, with many of the local schools taking part and famous athletes, such as Don Thompson, joining in; Thursday was procession night, when floats and individuals were cheered as they made their way through the streets to the park. On the last Saturday there was a variety of acts and events in the afternoon, which was partly repeated in the evening, resulting in a grand finale with military bands marching under spotlights shining down from towers specially built for the occasion. Many of the 'overspill' people, who had settled into their new homes, had never seen a carnival and the joyful spirit helped to bring a conciliation between the locals and the newcomers in those early years.

With the influx of new firms, as well as residents, the post office had to employ more postmen to deliver the extra mail to the new homes, offices and other businesses, with the result that more 'Walks' had to be added to the town delivery service. During the hard winters of the late 1950s and the freeze-up of 1963 the postmen found the going rather difficult. But there was the funny side of life, as in the case of one postman who sneezed so hard that his false teeth flew into a snowdrift. He made a mental note of where they landed and, when the thaw came, he was able to find them quite easily. On another occasion, a postman set light to a house when he pushed a roll of magazines through the letterbox knocking over a paraffin heater just inside the door. Luckily the quick action of the resident prevented a serious blaze. However, the most comical incident occurred when a postman, cycling back to town from his round, had his postman's cap set alight by a discarded cigarette end, thrown carelessly from a passing lorry. It was only when he stopped at the traffic lights in Chapel Street that he realised that he was on fire, when a lady paused to tell him there was smoke coming out of his cap! The thick waterproof lining inside had prevented his head from being burnt.

Humorous incidents occurred to policemen as well in those far off days. One policeman, whose duties were mainly on motor-bike, noticed a small fire burning by a roadside stretch of grass. The flames could have been put out with one stamp of the foot, but instead he decided to call the fire brigade on his radio. When the firemen got there they found the policeman trying to keep the fire going for them to put it out!

In 1961 the Southampton-based newspaper *The Southern Evening Echo* opened an office in Cross Street, Basingstoke, with a local edition of the publication. Later, a larger office was opened in Church Street, opposite the local weekly newspaper office of the *Hants and Berks Gazette*, and it was from there that news was collected by a team of reporters and sent to Southampton, for publication, each week day. By mid-afternoon a van delivered the newspapers to the local office, where any additional 'stop press' news was quickly printed. Then the papers were distributed to the various newsagents in the town.

The *Hants and Berks Gazette*, established in 1878 by the Bird family, was acquired by Purnell and Sons of Somerset in 1963; then two years later the Purnell and Hazell-Sun Groups merged to form the British Printing Corporation. The *Gazette* became an associate of B.P.C. but the local directors remained in control. In 1955, new presses had been installed and in the same year the news was printed on the front page for the first time. Up until then, except on outstanding occasions, the front page contained only advertisements. Situated in upper Church Street, the newspaper office was inside a small complex of buildings with a stationery shop in front. The printing works was at the rear adjoining Windover Street, a narrow lane at the rear of Church Street.

The 1960s saw the demise of one of the most outstanding features of the town—the large expanse of greenhouses along the Winchester Road and Cranbourne Lane, known as the Basingstoke Joint Nurseries. The west side of Basingstoke had several nurseries, especially at Kempshott and Worting. One of the earliest was set up by Mr. Brooks in 1902, in Roman Road, in conjunction with his grocery shop in London Street. Another was established in Pack Lane in 1935, by Mr. V. Rivaz, and the Ayling family's nurseries opened in Roman Road in 1948. But the combined greenhouses that spread across the land of Winchester Road were the largest, and from the playing fields of Fairfields School, overlooking the huge site, the whole area looked like 'a sea of glass'. In October 1960 the directors of the Joint Nurseries announced that the business would have to close, due to high production costs and the shortage of skilled labour. Work began on the dismantling of the buildings and the mass of glass which made up the greenhouses on the site.

The promise of a newly developed Basingstoke brought about an influx of firms who wanted to take advantage of the many industrial sites and units. Firms such as Merrivale Press, Wella Rapid, Pilcon, John Kimbell, and Charles Blatchford, established themselves in the town, alongside many others. But to some local businesses the prospect of seeing their years of hard work destroyed to make way for the new town centre was too much, and they closed several years before their buildings were due to be demolished. Mr. Albert Botting, the leather cutter of Potters Lane, closed his shop in 1961, while the Misses Philpott, who ran a confectionery shop two doors away, moved out in September 1964. But some firms were eager to settle into their new abode, such as John Carter's, the tent-makers, who left their Wote Street shop for larger premises in Winchester Road.

The Development Group, based in Cliddesden Road, intended to demolish the old town centre as from November 1966, but during 1964 local contractors were called upon to start work the following year. Even in 1964 part of Basing Road was cleared, and the old Eastrop Cottages were also pulled down. On 31 January 1965 the *Goat Inn*, in Goat Lane, closed down, and within six months had been cleared for the New Market Place, where some local shopkeepers were re-housed. Chapel Street and Bunnian Place, near the railway station, were also the scene of activity by demolition contractors, and one of the first buildings to go was the Soper's Almhouses, next to the Chapel Street bridge, which dated from 1891. In September 1965 Buckskin Farm closed down, while Chineham Farm was vacated in the following month.

On 17 October 1965 hundreds of people attended a special farewell service at the Church Street Methodist church. Among the audience were the mayor of Basingstoke and members of the local council, and five ministers who had been connected with the church in the past. It was a sad occasion for all those present, as many of them had seen the building badly damaged in the war and then restored after much hard work. Within a year the church was cleared of its fittings and in December 1966 it was completely demolished.

Meanwhile the influx of new firms continued, such as Mucon, Bell and Howell, Cannon Electric, Douglas Rownson, Lennox Heating, and many more during 1965. At Houndmills industrial estate one of the largest buildings of that time was erected—the warehouse and factory of J. Sainsbury Ltd., the firm whose grocery and provision shops were scattered all over the country. The depot covered seven and a half acres, and organised the daily distribution of goods to the many shops in southern England.

1965 saw the prelude to the vast development of Basingstoke and the last year of trade for most of the shopkeepers and other small businesses in the town. To the hundreds of residents who lived in the streets due for demolition the following year it was to be the last Christmas in their homes. For some of those who lived in May Street the move would mean better sanitary conditions and central heating, but to many others it meant the breaking-up of their community. It was the same in other areas, such as Gashouse Road, Bunnian Place, Clifton Terrace and roads where local folk had lived in harmony for decades. Some families found new homes elsewhere. As they were handed the meagre compensation money, so they moved away to places which were like Basingstoke as it was in the olden days. Small towns in Dorset, Surrey, Berkshire, and Somerset were selected, while some travelled even further away, such as to Staffordshire and Yorkshire. One man who had finished paying for his house and had just retired was so incensed with the thought that the family would have to leave that he tried to organise a petition to stop the demolition. But he failed to prevent the inevitable and he moved away to the north of England where property prices were cheaper. To all those who had lived through the war years, had seen the revival of the peacetime days, and then faced the transformation of their small market town into an area of housing estates, industrial sites, and new roads, Christmas 1965 posed problems about their future in Basingstoke. Over the following years they were to find out. Some liked the new town, others did not. The disappearance of the old town is best summed up in the words of one local character—'I miss the old town—it had charm and it had character'.

86. The view from the old Town Hall clock tower in 1958, showing the area of Basingstoke that was later demolished to make way for the new shopping centre. In the centre of the photograph is the white tower of the Savoy cinema in lower Wote Street, whilst close by are the firms of Wallis and Steevens and Gerrish, Ames, and Simpkins.

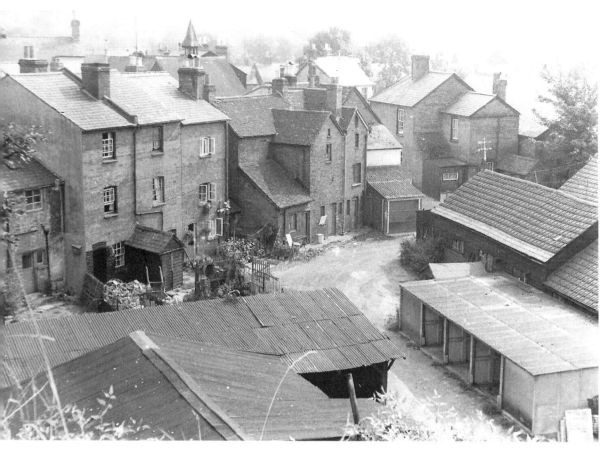

87. Part of the old Steam Dell at the rear of Reading Road. It was here that the town's original waterworks was established in 1871, but, after the typhoid epidemic of 1905 caused by pollution of the water supply, the present waterworks was set up at West Ham.

88. In 1945 Mr. Horace Carey, a local shopkeeper, suggested that Church Square be turned into War Memorial Gardens. This scene shows the War Memorial Gardens shortly after opening in 1956. It was difficult to believe that only 15 years before this was the site of so many private homes, bombed on that August day in 1940. A garden for the blind was also laid out in Church Square, opposite.

89. The end of the Second World War witnessed an increase in road traffic, and the problem of parking vehicles in the town became acute. Therefore, the land at the rear of New Road and London Street was cleared in 1957 to make way for the central car park.

90. In the late 1950s buildings on the corner of London Street and New Road were demolished to facilitate traffic access. New Road was quite narrow at this point in those days, and with the increase of vehicles through the town there was a need to keep traffic moving.

91. New Street in the mid-1950s. The large building once housed the antique business of Antonio Dellafera. The business closed down *c*.1958 and during demolition a few years later the huge chimney stack crashed with such force into the cellar that the town centre literally shook from the vibrations. In the background of the picture can be seen the small shops belonging to the Basingstoke Co-operative Society.

92. Hackwood Road in the late 1950s. The shop on the right was run by Mr. and Mrs. Weaver and was known as the Toll House Kiosk (a toll house had formerly stood on the site). The Kiosk was a popular place for the many people who attended functions held in the War Memorial Gardens, especially the annual carnivals.

93. A row of shops in New Street, all owned by the Co-operative Society, was demolished in November 1961 to make way for a large store, which was completed the following year. Within 24 years the store closed and in 1985 the large building was pulled down and an office block built in its place.

94. Father Christmas calls at Curry's electrical shop in London Road, 1956, long before decimalisation was to change the price tickets in the shops. Some eleven years after the war ended, goods such as toys were becoming increasingly available, and the days of restrictions owing to lack of metal and other materials were becoming just a memory. For these children the war was just a mention in their school history books.

95. Members of the St John Ambulance Service march through the streets of Basingstoke during one of the annual remembrance parades in the 1950s. In those days nearly every group in the town took part—boy scouts, police, firemen, girl guides, and many more, whilst hundreds of people stood in the streets to watch them go by. The service at the War Memorial Park was also well attended, whatever the weather, by the Mayor and Corporation and other dignitaries.

96. The British Legion flags are dipped during the two minutes' silence at the War Memorial Park during the latter years of the 1950s. In the background stand the Municipal Buildings.

97. Hanging up the bunting in upper Church Street for the annual carnival week in the late 1950s. Vernon Griffiths' house furnishing shop, on the left, was established in 1902 at 17 Church Street, then moved to larger premises further along Church Street. Mr. Griffiths died in 1939 leaving the business to his sons. Next door were the offices of the Southern Gas Board, while further down the road can be seen what was then the *Black Boy* hotel, which was renamed the *Hop Leaf*.

98. Miss Jean Noyce, the carnival queen for 1956. When it was decided to hold a new series of carnivals in Basingstoke that year, a contest to find a queen was held at the Haymarket Theatre. The funds from the following carnivals went towards the building of the Carnival Hall, at Fairfields, which was erected in 1964.

99. Dancing in the streets during the Mardi Gras of 1958's Basingstoke Carnival. This was a popular event at the carnival, and attracted people from miles around. Winchester Street and London Street were closed to traffic, as well as upper Church Street and Wote Street, to allow people plenty of freedom for their dancing. The band played in front of the Town Hall and the music could be heard from quite a distance.

100. Some of the many people who helped to collect money for the annual carnivals in the 1950s. This was the scene in the War Memorial Park during the interval in the Grand Finale on the last night of the week's events, when up to five bands would take part.

101. The band of the Royal Marines in the War Memorial Park during the grand finale on Saturday evening of carnival week in 1958. Hundreds of people from all over the South of England enjoyed the sound and spectacle of the music, marching and spotlights.

102. Santa Claus and the children of the staff of the Wilts and Dorset Bus Company at their Christmas party in the late 1950s. On this enjoyable occasion the biggest laugh came after the photographer fell off the chair he was standing on, after taking this picture.

103. The scene in the centre of Basingstoke in the 1950s, with the market in front of the Town Hall and two-way traffic flowing along Winchester Street and into London Street. The policeman on point duty helped traffic to come out of Wote Street. In July 1960 a one-way system was introduced, which allowed traffic to head west along Southern Road and east through the town centre.

104. Mr. and Mrs. McCallum in their newsagent's shop in Church Street, shortly after acquiring it from G. Stevens Ltd. in the 1950s. They sold a large range of sweets, cigarettes and tobacco as well as stocks of stationery and greetings cards. At a time when there were few magazines, they were able to spread them out on the counter, although there were more newspapers than there are now.

105. The Waldorf cinema, in lower Wote Street, on the occasion of the 'Dunkirk' film being shown in 1958. Prior to the film, a small military parade took place in the road outside, and the cinema was decorated for the event. The cinema was built in 1935 by Mr. Casey with a seating capacity of 863, and originally with a square screen, but this was redesigned in 1953 for the cinemascope film 'The Robe'. In very wet weather the lower part of the interior would be flooded, and the stalls had to be dried out.

106. A train gets steam up to travel from Basingstoke railway station to Winchester in the late 1950s. The steam engines were to last another decade before electric and diesel trains arrived on the scene. The picture was taken with the permission of the pharmaceutical firm Eli Lilly, who later built an extension on the land to the right of this photograph.

107. Some of the Wilts and Dorset buses parked on the old Basingstoke canal land in lower Wote Street in the late 1950s. Until recently the buses had no doors to keep out the cold during the winter months, which must have been uncomfortable for the driver and the conductor. In 1962 a bus station was built on the site in preparation for the increase in the town's population.

108. Lower Wote Street in the late 1950s with Station Hill in the background. On the right is the Waldorf cinema, built in 1935 and closed down in 1991. The whole of the left-hand side was demolished to make way for the new town centre in 1967.

109. Watson's Garage in Wote Street, in 1962, were established *c*.1900. They were agents for Vauxhall, Daimler, Lanchester, Land Rover and Jaguar cars, and dealt with a large range of repairs as well. Their stores kept a wide variety of spares and accessories, some of which dated back to their early years in business.

110. A 1950s view across Loddon Valley from London Road, with the gasworks in the distance. In the foreground are the private houses of Allnutt Avenue, whilst the nearby field now contains the Riverdene housing estate.

111. Merton Farm, off Aldermaston Road, in the late 1950s. Having had much of its land acquired for housing in the 1920s, and further acreage taken in the early 1950s for industrial purposes, the farm ran down its stock of famous shorthorn pedigree cows, and in 1961 closed down its dairy.

112. A scene from *Pirates of Penzance*, one of the many shows performed by the local operatic society at the Haymarket Theatre in the 1950s and '60s. One of the leading singers of that time was Anne Jeffries (left), who had previously sung on the radio in the Carol Levis Show, and had been singing since she was a young girl. She died at Nottingham in April 1994, aged 78.

113. The Youth Club at the Methodist Church in Sarum Hill in the late 1950s. Alan Spencer, the club leader is on the left, and the Rev. Lake, the church minister is (top) second from right. At a time when the youth of the country were needing more attention, Basingstoke was opening up new fields for them in the form of clubs and organisations. This particular club, in the hall at the rear of the church, was adequately provided with games, puzzles, and speakers in the winter and plenty of outdoor activities in the summer.

114. Winchester Road, seen from the Alton Light Railway bridge, in the late 1950s. The land on the left was often rented to fun fairs and circuses until it was used for industrial purposes. In the background is the factory of Kelvin and Hughes, previously known as Kelvin, Bottomley & Baird.

115. Church Street at the junction with Cross Street in the late 1950s, with the Warren newsagents in the foreground, and further up the road Tom Cooper's chemist's shop.

116. New Street, *c.*1956. The Camera Centre originally operated from a small shop in Mortimer Lane in the late 1950s, before moving to New Street as business increased. Both the Camera Centre and Majorca restaurant closed down some years later.

117. Buckland Avenue, on the Berg Estate, during its construction in 1958. Named after the developers E. and L. Berg of Esher, Surrey, the estate was nicknamed the Garden Estate. Most of the buildings were bungalows, but a few houses were built close to the Winchester Road. Prices varied from £1,765 to £2,495, the average deposit being £200 and the weekly repayment was about £2.

18. The upkeep of local garden nurseries in the late 1950s became so expensive that many were forced to close. One of the largest, Cranbourne Nurseries, brought its business to an end in 1960 and the site later became Cranbourne Secondary school. This scene shows the dismantling of the greenhouses in Cranbourne Lane.

19. The circus comes to town! This is the scene in the late 1950s when the elephants were walked through the town to Winchester Road, where the circus tent was being raised. In the background is the railway station, while the building to the right is the side of the Cattle Market. When the elephants were unloaded one local man, Mr. Tomlin, an estate agent, stated that he had returned from an African holiday and did not see one elephant—until he got back to Basingstoke!

120. One day in the late 1950s there was much activity by firemen in Basingstoke Market Place. A 'bubble-car' was found to be on fire, caused by a cigarette end being left on the seat. The fire was soon put out and the town centre returned to normal. These three-wheeled runabouts were popular at the time; the Isetta and other models sold for around £350.

121. Basingstoke and North Hants. cricket club in action at May's Bounty, Bounty Road, in 1960. John May—who was mayor of Basingstoke several times—was a great benefactor to the town. He bought the cricket ground to prevent it being sold to a local builder for housing. Cricket was a popular pastime and was even played during the war, although there were difficulties with transport and the provision of food, due to rationing. In the post-war years the club lost several of its members, including its president, Rex Lamb, who died in 1955, followed by his replacement, Mr. T. C. Chesterfield, who died in 1956.

122. The bleakness of the winter of 1960 is reflected in this scene at Merton Farm, off the Kingsclere Road. The farm, like others on the outskirts of Basingstoke, was eventually taken over for redevelopment, and a new road system and industrial units have now been built on the site.

123. Roseneath Cottages in Hackwood Road in the 1950s. The cottages were demolished to make way for the New Road extension, which now winds its way round to Victoria Street. At the rear of these houses was Thomas Burberry's factory, where thousands of his famous coats were manufactured from 1892 until 1957, after which it transferred to London.

124. Crowds of people waiting for the start of the carnival motor-cycle scramble on the fields near Kingsclere Road, c.1959—now the site of the Houndmills Industrial estate which was to be built within a few years.

125. This long line of traffic through Winchester Street into London Street, was caused by a hold up in traffic along the Basingstoke Bypass due to the Easter horse races at Hackwood Park. The races were held annually on land close to the London Road near Old Basing. To avoid the jam, motorists would often drive into the town, only to find that a similar problem confronted them in the town centre.

126. One of the many shows performed at the May Place Hall in the 1950s and '60s. Built in 1907 for the use of the nearby Congregational Church (later the United Reform Church), the building was added to in 1928. During the war it was used by the military for various purposes, but is now used as offices, after being sold by the church.

127. Mr. Stevens, jnr., helping his mother at the fish and chip shop in lower Wote Street in the early 1960s. Established in 1908 by Mr. W. C. Stevens, the shop included a small room at the rear for people to sit and enjoy their food on the premises. The fryer was one of the few coal-heating-operated fryers still in operation.

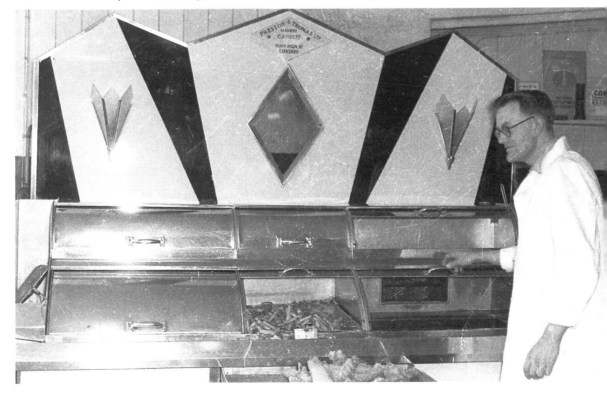

128. Bramblys Grange House prior to its demolition, *c*.1965, and the erection of the present-day health centre and surgeries. The old mansion was, for many years, the home of Mr. Thomas Thornycroft, the founder of the engineering factory in Basingstoke.

129. The West Ham swimming pool, *c*.1965. Situated close to the waterworks, it was opened to the public in 1906. Until it closed down some 60 years later, the pool was used by various schools and organisations. The Alton Light Railway ran close by between 1901 and 1936, the embankment of which remained until the 1960s.

130. The scene on 24 July 1960 when a one-way road system was started through Winchester Street, London Street, Southern Road and Victoria Street. The picture shows traffic heading east along London Street towards the New Road and Hackwood Road crossroads.

131. Dismantling the Town Hall clock tower in November 1961. Shortly before this picture was taken the photographer nearly plunged from the extended scaffolding planks some 100 ft. into the Market Place. As he stepped backwards to get the scene in his viewfinder, one of the workmen shouted out 'Don't go back any further mate!', and saved him from crippling injuries.

132. Demolition of the Winchester Road bridge in 1961. Built in 1901 for the Alton Light Railway, it became a danger to high vehicles, especially buses, after the railway closed down in 1936.

133. The demolition of the Alton Light Railway bridge at Cliddesden on the night of 1 December 1962. The work took place on one of the coldest nights of the year and continued right through to the early hours of Sunday morning to remove the 61-year-old bridge which bore the track of the Alton to Basingstoke line until its closure.

134. Church Street in 1962, showing the Conservative Club on the left. Within a few years all these buildings were demolished for the new town centre. Most of the shopkeepers closed their businesses and never re-opened, although a few found alternative shops in or around the town.

135. The Church Street Methodist church, and the County Court offices, in the early 1960s. The offices were also used by various solicitors, such as those employed by Kingdon and Seldon, and Bayley and Mant, both of whom had to find alternative offices when the building was demolished in 1966.

136. New Road in the early 1960s. The building on the left was the Basingstoke Ex-Servicemen's Club. Originally known as the Victory Club when it was established in 1919, it later became the British Legion. The new name was inaugurated in 1955. The building was later altered and extended into its present shape.

137. An aerial view of Station Hill in the early 1960s, showing the large factory complex of Wallis and Steevens, the engineering firm, on the right-hand side. The clothing manufacturers, Gerrish, Ames and Simpkins, are situated on the other side of the road, on the left. The *Barge Inn*, with its yard used by Stowell's Taxis, is in the lower left-hand corner.

138. The *Victory Inn*, on the junction of Essex Road and Brook Street, in the 1960s. The public house became synonymous with the game of darts, as the venue for the local championships. One name from those days, still very much remembered locally, is Bert Kelly. He reached the finals of the darts championships for England and Wales in 1958, after winning the local finals.

139. Winchester Street in the 1960s, with Milwards shoe shop (left) soon after it was refitted. After the discontinuation of the shoe repair service, the shop was able to provide more room to display the many new types of platform and stiletto shoes which were popular at the time.

140. Junction Road in the early 1960s. Situated between Chapel Street and Station Hill, the road consisted mainly of terraced houses built in the 1870s. The corner shop on the left was a newsagent's popular with people going to Eli Lilly's factory and other industrial places in Kingsclere Road. The area was demolished in the 1960s for town development.

141. In January 1963 heavy snow brought traffic to a halt in the Basingstoke area, and on the Winchester Road, at the top of Kempshott Hill, one motorist became stuck up to his bonnet. The snow arrived on Boxing Day 1962 but it was weeks before it finally cleared, the worst fall of snow since 1947.

142. In May 1963 an Aldershot and District bus accidentally pulled over the scaffolding on the front of W. H. Smith's in the Market Place. It was feared that it would fall on the market and passers-by, but the fire service quickly dismantled the poles and planks before any further damage was done.

143. The Basingstoke Carnival Queen of 1960, Miss Althea Preston, gives a cheerful smile to Mr. Jack Welling, the chairman of the carnival committee, and the many onlookers in the War Memorial Park, where most of the activities took place.

144. Some hundreds of people gathered to see the carnival procession in London Street, c.1960. In the background, to the left, are Deane's Almshouses, to the rear of which extensions were being built at the time.

145. 'Pip' Robotham and his pop group in the early 1960s. One of many similar groups formed at the time, when the youth of the country enjoyed the beat of modern music, from skiffle to rock 'n' roll.

146. The scene at one of the '7.5 Special' shows in the town, when local groups showed off their talents. Many shows were organised by Prince Star Entertainments who gave to various local charities large amounts of money from the profits. The shows were held at various places including Park Prewett and the Shrubbery School.

147. Dancing the twist during a competition at the Shrubbery Girls' School in 1962. This was one of many functions held in the town during the early days of rock and roll and other dances such as the twist, the shuffle, and the locomotion.

148. The Vine hunt moves from the market place after assembling on Boxing Day 1967—the last meet prior to amalgamation with the Craven hunt. Founded in 1790, this hunt was a traditional and familiar scene in north Hampshire, attracting hundreds of people, especially children. During the Second World War it closed down, but in 1949 it reopened after land at Hannington village was purchased for kennels and stables. No meets were held in Basingstoke after 1967.

149. Road widening in Winchester Road, at its junction with Pack Lane, in the early 1960s. The work was necessary because of the number of accidents caused by cars speeding down Kempshott Hill and colliding with oncoming vehicles. In the background, to the right, is the Tower Café, now the site of Sainsbury's Homebase store.

150. The Mayor and Corporation attending the annual Remembrance Day service at the War Memorial Park. This picture was taken in 1962 when Cllr. John Peat was Mayor. To his left was the Town Clerk, Mr. Roger Purvis, while among the councillors present were John Stroud, Cyril Wood and Walter Evans.

151. The mayor of Basingstoke, Cllr. Townsend, and the carnival queen, Barbara Deane, shake hands with the T.V. All-Stars at Whiteditch Playing Fields in 1961, when they came to Basingstoke to play football against 'Pember's Pensioners', a team of local footballers. Organised by the carnival committee, the stars of stage, screen, radio and T.V. helped to keep the locals laughing during an afternoon of thundery rain. Among the stars were Bernard Bresslaw and Larry Taylor.

152. A group of youths in the early 1960s at the War Memorial Park. The fashion then was for longer jackets, 'Italian' style trousers and hair styles which copied that of Elvis Presley.

153. A gathering of Technical College students, *c*.1964, after taking part in their 'Rag Week', an annual event for the college, in which the students carried out various activities for fund-raising. One year they pushed a bedstead round the streets of the town, and another year they removed the flagpole from the front of the rural district council offices. The cork from the champagne bottle has been 'frozen' in mid-air.

154. The mayor and mayoress of Basingstoke of 1962—Councillor John Peat and his wife—with his daughter Judith, and the Pearly King and Princess of Basingstoke. The picture was taken during a lull in the carnival week's events.

155. The Venture Restaurant alongside the Basingstoke bypass in the early 1960s. Named after the Venture Bus company, it was next to the Venture Service station (a petrol filling station), and both were close to the Venture Roundabout. The latter was one of the first roundabouts to be built in Basingstoke, in 1931. In recent years, the town has been given the nickname 'doughnut city' as it has acquired so many roundabouts.

156. The War Memorial Park children's playground in the 1960s. This was one of many facilities in the park for the locals to enjoy. With bowling, tennis, football and other sports, the park was the venue for amusement and entertainment. Unfortunately the removal of the bowling and tennis areas to build the new council offices has meant that this part of the War Memorial Park has little to offer.

157. The new Penrith Road extension area shortly after its completion in 1960. This was once the site of Jordan's Nurseries, with its large area of greenhouses and water tower. During the construction of the road certain problems arose due to subsidence caused by the boggy land.

158. Christmas in the early 1960s. Decorations were placed on the Town Hall and a tree provided and installed in the Market Place. The clock on the front of the building was fitted in 1963, two years after the clock tower was dismantled.

159. Wallis and Steevens factory, Station Hill, in the early 1960s. It was a large complex of buildings which grew from a small business established in the mid-19th century, originally as Wallis and Haslam. Among the many agricultural machines made by the firm were steam rollers, some of which were exported all over the world.

160. The local Caledonian Society enjoying their annual social in 1963 at the Basingstoke Town Hall. The Town Hall was used by various organisations for meetings, dances and other functions, but this constant use by crowds of people caused weaknesses in the upper and lower floors. In 1981 the local council decided to sell the building and two years later it became the Willis Museum.

161. The Savoy cinema in lower Wote Street. Built just prior to the start of the Second World War, it replaced a smaller cinema, the Electric, which had operated since 1910—one of the first cinemas in Hampshire. As the fire station was just yards away, audiences at the Savoy often had to contend with the siren blasting during the film performances.

162. Wote Street in the early 1960s. The Crofts stores was originally Forrest stores, which sold groceries and wine and spirits. Like several other stores in the town, payment by customers was sent up to the cash office via a tramline system in special screw-on cups, and any change was returned the same way, which fascinated the children.

163. Hackwood Road, close to the Basingstoke Bypass, before it was made into a dual carriageway for the Town Development Scheme in the mid-1960s. Private houses were built on the land on the left.

164. Lower Church Street in the early 1960s, with Mr. Porter's jewellery shop in the foreground. Further down the road was Mr. Shorney's paint shop and the Conservative Club, which was established in 1885 in Cross Street before transferring to Church Street in 1909.

165. Basingstoke Technical College shortly after its completion in Worting Road in 1960. The design and construction cost £211,450 and further extensions and alterations have since taken place.

166. The Shrubbery Maternity Home in Cliddesden Road in the 1960s. The old Shrubbery mansion, where Thomas Burberry, the raincoat manufacturer, used to live, was acquired by Hampshire County Council in 1947. It became a maternity home to ease the pressure on the Hackwood Road Cottage Hospital at a time when there was a sudden increase in the birth rate soon after the end of the war. It was demolished in 1993.

167. The Methodist church at the top of Sarum Hill. The building was demolished in July 1970, having stood for 68 years. A new church was built further down the hill in the same year, after the demolition of a row of houses. The church had a band in the pre-war period and this became the Basingstoke Silver Band in 1941.

168. Christmas at the post office was always a busy time, especially in the sorting office during the post-war years, and visitors often called in to see how the work was going on. In the early 1960s Denzil Freeth (left), the local Member of Parliament, paid a visit and was shown around by Mr. Blachford, the Head Postmaster of Basingstoke.

169. In November 1965 a goods train lost a truck over the Chapel Street embankment after crashing through the buffers. This happened in the evening, causing traffic chaos as the police closed the road for several hours. By the morning the rest of the train had been removed, leaving the wreckage of the truck for all to see. (Luckily the houses on the site had been demolished just months before.)

170. Construction of the Riverdene housing estate in the early 1960s. This land used to be Goldings Farm, which was associated with Goldings Park, renamed the War Memorial Park in 1921.

171. The first meeting at the Town Hall to discuss the impending Town Development Scheme, in August 1962. With a population increase from 26,000 to 75,000 being anticipated, the scheme involved the demolition of some 55 houses, 46 shops, seven public houses, a school, a church, fire station, two factories and a cinema to make way for the new shopping centre.

172. May Street, one of the roads destined to disappear under the Town's Development Scheme. Built in the 1880s, this long and straight road, mainly of terraced houses, was to give the local council a problem when it came to re-housing the many people living there. Families who had lived close to each other for years wanted to stay together, but this proved difficult.

173. *The Railway Arms* public house in Brook Street was originally an 18th-century building that was converted to an inn, *c*.1840. It was one of the many inns to be demolished in the new town centre clearance.

174. Mrs. M. Jarvis (seated on the left) on the night of the closure of her public house, *The Goat*, in Goat Lane, February 1965. Seventy-year-old Mrs. Jarvis closed the doors having been proprietress there for 35 years. Her nephew had helped to run the business since her husband's death in 1962. In June 1965 the building was demolished to make way for the New Market Place, and five months later Mrs. Jarvis passed away.

175. The last service held at the Church Street Methodist Church in October 1965. Among the many parishioners upset by the plans to demolish the church for town development were Mr. William Champion, who had been in the choir for 60 years, and Mrs. F. Peach, who was the first baby to be christened at the church on its opening in 1906 and whose mother was the last person to have a funeral at the church in 1965.